Start Fast!

How to accelerate your software / internet / mobile venture

by Chuck Stormon

DEDICATION

To the divine source of inspiration and those with the perseverance to see it through to realization. And to Steve, Arthur, Albert and Samuel.

"Your time is limited, so don't waste it living someone else's life. Don't be trapped by dogma, which is living with the results of other people's thinking. Don't let the noise of others' opinions drown out your own inner voice, heart and intuition. They somehow already know what you truly want to become. Everything else is secondary."
– Steven P. Jobs

"Any sufficiently advanced technology is indistinguishable from magic."
– Arthur C. Clarke

"Anyone who has never made a mistake has never tried anything new."
– Albert Einstein

"The harder I work, the luckier I get."
- Samuel Goldwyn

CONTENTS

Chuck Stormon

ACKNOWLEDGMENTS

This book (not to mention my career) would not have been possible without all the co-founders, mentors, investors, co-workers, customers, partners, clients and friends I've been privileged to spend time with over the last 25 years. I am truly grateful for all of my experiences with them - especially the difficult ones, for these are the ones from which I probably learned the most.

INTRODUCTION

"My suggestion is that you go home. At the back door they will give you your money back and you can go home now and not get started on this very difficult and terrible process. It is a lot more difficult than you know when you begin. Once you start it is very difficult to stop. So my suggestion to you is not to begin. Best not to start at all. But if you do, then it is best to finish."
- Chogyam Trungpa Rinpoche

This book is for anyone starting a software, mobile or internet business, for first time or serial entrepreneurs, for investors and for friends, family and loved ones who want to better understand the entrepreneurs in their lives.

This is not a feel-good introduction, designed to pump you up with excitement and confidence. This is not the kind of introduction designed to get you to buy/read/share this book. I'm going to do something very unusual, almost radical. I'm going to tell you the truth.

Most books on starting a company begin by telling you about the great success stories. I'm going to begin by trying to talk you out of it. If I fail to talk you out of it in this Introduction then read the rest of the book.

Why do you want to start a company? You should examine this. Sit with it. Write down your reasons. Are any of these reasons on your list?

- Entrepreneurs get rich and I want to be rich.

- In today's world of global economic crisis, my job could be on the line at any given moment so starting my own business isn't any riskier.

- One of the greatest perks about owning my own company is that I get to be my own boss.

- Starting a company will give me the freedom to set my own hours and schedule so I will be able to enjoy a lot of time off, work at my own leisure, spend a lot of time with my family and friends and create a life that I enjoy.

- I want to turn my passion into my livelihood. Doing what I love for a living will make me fulfilled and enrich my life.

- I want a more relaxed work environment where everyone can be friends.

In fact the above are the six *worst* reasons to do a startup. These myths and lies came from a recent article published on the Small Business Administration website, from which I paraphrased these 6 bullet points.

The truth is that only some entrepreneurs get rich. Many spend their life savings and that of family and friends and fail anyway.

Yes the economy stinks right now, and it will probably get worse before it gets better. If you have a job, it is best to keep it as long as you can. More people have become well-off by getting a regular paycheck, living within their means, and saving and investing for the long term.

If your startup succeeds, you won't be your own boss. There are investors, boards of directors and don't forget your customers. And oh, yeah, you'll probably be replaced soon by a boss brought in by your investors to run "your" business.

As for more leisure, that's a laugh! Running a business is a 24×7 endeavor. There is no way around it; it's just plain hard. Expect stress, less hair, exhaustion, ruined relationships, you name it. In the pressure-cooker of starting a business you may completely forget what you loved about the idea in the first place.

What about a relaxed, friendly work environment? Not very likely. You will be the focus of everyone's projections. Your co-workers will love you one day and hate you the next. Expect to deal with difficult, brutal, no-win people problems, threatened and real lawsuits, and heartbreaking reversals of fortune.

In case you're not convinced, here are some more reasons NOT to start a company.

1. It's up to you. There is no one else to blame for poor performance or failure to execute.

2. Where will you get the money you'll need to grow the business? Banks aren't lending to and venture capitalists aren't investing in early-stage startups.

3. I wouldn't advise anyone with a family to found a startup. If you have a family, they will suffer with you. If single 20-somethings start a company that fails, so what? They'll learn a lot, and can still get a job. If you've got a spouse and a couple of toddlers, you've got too much to lose.

So sit with this decision and be sure, because starting down this road you're taking a step onto a slippery slope. If you find that you *can* avoid starting a business then do. If, on the other hand you, like me, *can't not do it*, well then you might as well do it right. Go ahead and read the rest of the book.

CHAPTER 1 - START FAST

"Start fast, that's the biggest thing. Start fast."
- Ohio State senior defensive end Solomon Thomas

Hi, my name is Chuck and I'm an addict. To be more precise, I'm addicted to starting companies. People more polite than myself call me a serial entrepreneur. I've spent the last 25 years starting companies, learning what to do and what not to do, being mentored and mentoring others.

The single biggest thing I've learned in all these years is how to start fast, which I believe is the best way to build a software, internet or mobile app business today. In the few hours it takes you to read this book I'm going to share with you what it took me 25 years to figure out.

Of course reading about it is not enough. So throughout the book you will find these little grey action boxes, which give you something specific and practical to do.

> **<u>Go to a Startup Weekend</u>**: (<u>startupweekend.org</u>), commit to the entire 54 hours and experience in microcosm what it's like to do a startup. By the way, I recommend this for everyone, not just first-timers. This will give you an opportunity to practice the concepts in this book and see for yourself. It's also a great way to network and meet potential co-founders, partners, sponsors, and investors in your community.

There are tremendous advantages to a fast start. You'll be able to see your idea in action quickly, get feedback from early adopters, adapt your product or service in response to that feedback, test and refine your business model all before investing a lot of money (yours or someone else's).

I'm going to give you a method, specific tools and action steps to start fast, build a real business fast and attain as much success as possible in the least time and with the least capital. Bear in mind that this method will not be applicable to every business. Not every business can be capital-efficient. Some take longer to build than others. I know that this method applies to a business if it is software-based and your customers can be reached through the Internet or mobile phone network. If your business is of a different character entirely, some but not everything here will apply to you.

There are reasons that software, internet and mobile companies can start fast, and most of these reasons are obvious once you know them. But most of them weren't true 10 years ago, some five years ago, and a few weren't true only 1 year ago. Here they are:

- More than two billion people (30% of the world) have access to the internet. That's a big market. This includes roughly 80% of the people in the North America and 60% of the people in Europe. In Asia, only 25% of the population has internet access, but that accounts for almost a billion people.

- You can access your market directly. In the past it was difficult to break into markets. You had to know the right people, play politics, pay your dues. The Internet has led to the disintermediation (cutting out the middle-men) of every market it has touched (books, music, retail, travel, insurance, you name it). TV is going through this process of disintermediation and realignment right now. The Internet makes it much easier and faster to "break in" to almost any business.

- Thousands of developers have created an open source software stack which makes the development of new products and services much easier. This platform is available for free, further reducing your capital requirements.

- Cloud computing – ever heard of it? You can now rent everything you need to scale your online business. There are millions of servers and millions of lines of code available for the asking.

The next five chapters cover each of the five stages of starting a business[1]. Following the steps and using the tools in each chapter will ensure that you start fast.

Chapter 2 – Formation of your business. You'll need a team, a product or service idea, a business model and a value proposition.

Chapter 3 – Prototype your product or service to validate your value proposition and business model with real customers. You'll need to create a landing page, collect prospects, prototype your product, sign and get feedback from early adopters.

Chapter 4 – Iterate - Promote, validate, and adjust your startup product and business model. Iterate until you have traction. This is the drumbeat of a fast start. Get good at it and you'll build a successful business.

---

[1] This book presents my adaptation of the Lean Startup method, which means reducing waste by maximizing contact with real customers, testing assumptions as early as possible using rapid prototypes, evolving quickly using customer feedback and eliminating any work or investment that doesn't produce value for customers.

Chapter 5 – <u>Financing and Scaling</u> the business represent new challenges. You'll need to understand and carefully select investors who fit. You'll need to adapt as the needs of your business evolve.

Chapter 6 - <u>End Games</u> are the scenarios for you and your investors getting an economic return on all this work.

Throughout the book you will also find footnotes with personal stories from my entrepreneurial life as well as a few jokes and notes on additional reading. The first time you read this book you may find the footnotes illustrative, helpful and even entertaining. When you reread a chapter you can easily ignore them. The stories in the footnotes are not told in any chronological order. There is a timeline in the Epilogue that will help you sequence things if you're so inclined.

Please feel free to write in this book; make it your own. If you've got ideas for improvements, contribute them via <u>startfast.net</u> and I'll consider including them in the next revision.

Before we embark upon this journey, let me share a few words specifically with first-time entrepreneurs to help you set aside any unrealistic expectations you may be harboring.

Most people won't understand

> *"My son is an entrepreneur. That's what you call someone who is un-employed."*
> *- Ted Turner, founder of CNN and philanthropist*

Friends and family[2] will think you're nuts to give up your job to chase your startup dream. When you achieve major milestones in the startup process (e.g. getting first customers, raising capital, getting press) "normal" people won't get it or appreciate it. If you're not the next Facebook (and let's face it, most of us won't be), only others in the entrepreneurial ecosystem will understand what you're trying to do or why you would bother.

Long hours but the pay stinks

You will make less than normal wages for a while. If you got into entrepreneurship first and foremost for the money, then it's time to rethink. The day you sell your company and make a killing is a long way off. Until then, any extra cash you take in will go to growing the company, hiring the best team and building the platform rather than giving yourself a raise. You will

---

[2] The first time I started a company my mother tried to talk me out of it. Now, since I've managed to do well, she just says, "Oh that's nice." But does she actually know what I do for a living?

make less than most of your friends who took jobs for big companies and much less those who became accountants, attorneys or investment bankers.

Count me in for metric[3]

Everything takes much longer than you think it will or should. I developed a rule of thumb to help me estimate how long projects would actually take or cost versus what I thought they should. First gather your team's best estimates, throw out any outliers, average the rest, then double the result and add thirty percent. Works every time. A piece of software should take two weeks to develop, plan for five weeks. Your plan says you should be at break-even in six months, be prepared for 15 months of negative cash flow.

Nineteen 'no's for every yes.

In what other realm of life is a 95% failure rate normal? It is that way in sales and in a startup. Be prepared for a lot of rejection as you try to gain your first customers, raise capital, and form partnerships. Persistence is key, but so is trying new tactics until you crack the code. Most deals never work out – from acquisitions down to

---

[3] Remember Bob and Doug McKenzie from SCTV? "So how many beers in a metric six pack? Well, let's see. Double it and add thirty, eh? Six and six is twelve, plus 30 is 42 beers. Count me in for metric!"

simple sales agent agreements[4]. Deals fall through all the time. You should prepare for this eventuality and remember that for now you're your own best salesperson.

Titles are meaningless[5]

So you're the CEO, Chairman of the Board or Co-founder of a startup company. Just remember that titles mean nothing. Everyone is going to have to pitch in and do what they can. It is a grind, but it's also exhilarating. Business cards are nice to hand out at trade shows, but don't ever take yourself or your title too seriously. You have to do whatever needs doing.

You are the object of my projections

When you have employees, they will not love and respect you for who you are and what you've done. Generally, they will bring all their personal emotional "stuff" or "baggage" to work with them and project it on you. As the founder, you get to be a person with

---

[4] In my most recent startup I signed half a dozen independent sales agents to push business to business sales of our startup's products and services. Only one of the individuals ever actually sold anything.

[5] My first title in my first startup was "CEO and Chief Scientist." How impressive, right? I got to clean toilets, move racks of computers, crawl around in the ceiling and pull cables. And I loved every minute of it. Well not the toilets.

whom they work out their Mommy/Daddy issues. I have no advice for you. I just know it helps to have an idea where some of the crazy comes from when inappropriate, hurtful or downright nutty comments are coming at you.

So why am I doing this?

Don't ask me. Ask Tony Robbins. I'm just going to tell you how to do it fast and successfully. I'm glad I've worked for start-ups for 21 of the last 25 years and I'm grateful to have co-founded four of them. Once I started down this road I was hooked on the thrill of creating something from nothing through the pure effort and will that my co-founders and I could sustain. But why did I start the first company before I knew that? I'm not sure I had any choice in the matter[6].

---

[6] My first startup happened out of necessity. I was a PhD student leading a group of other graduate students to design a new kind of chip. One day our professor came by to let me know that he was leaving for a year to go on sabbatical in Cambridge UK. He also mentioned that the funding for our project was running out in 3 months and suggested I contact our sponsors for an extension.

When our sponsors told me that no funding was available to continue our work, I had to come up with an alternative. Starting a company seemed to be the only answer, and with an SBIR Grant from the US Department of Energy we were on our way.

Start fast or go home

If you're determined to start a software, internet or mobile app business, then the next few chapters will help you accelerate the process. If you're not really determined, then please go home. I won't think any less of you, I promise. You can still walk away at this point and save yourself a lot of heart-ache. If you do go on, don't say I didn't warn you.

To succeed at a startup (or anything else for that matter) you need to develop certain skills. One of the most fundamental of these is effective time management and here is one way to master it.

Time Management

> *"The key is not to prioritize what's on your schedule, but to schedule your priorities."*
> *- Stephen Covey, author and leadership trainer*

If you're like many entrepreneurs you may feel like you're constantly putting out fires. Here are three techniques for time management I call Triage, Touch It Once, and Priority Quadrant Analysis. Apply these tools regularly and you'll soon feel as though there are more hours in the day.

Triage – Not everything that comes your way needs your attention. You can quickly divide incoming tasks or requests into three groups: items for you to do, items to delegate to or collaborate on with someone else and items to trash. A quick mnemonic for this is Keep, Give Away, Throw Away.

<u>Touch it once</u> – When you do triage, you will encounter certain Keep items that can be taken care of immediately or in just a few seconds or minutes. Examples are returning a phone call, replying to an email, or paying a bill. Rather than putting these on the to-do list at all, just do them immediately so you only have to touch that task once. This way you avoid wasting time sorting and prioritizing trivial tasks. It's quicker just to get them done.

<u>Priority Quadrant Analysis</u> – this technique ensures that you're doing the most important things first.

Priority Quadrant Analysis

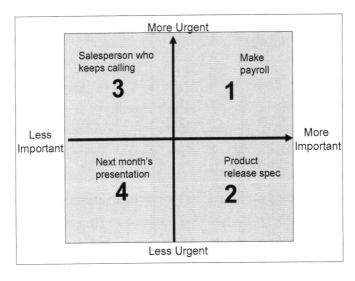

Chuck Stormon

> **<u>Create a Priority Quadrant Analysis</u>**: Draw
> two axes. The vertical axis runs from bottom to
> top - Less Urgent to More Urgent. The
> horizontal axis runs from left to right – Less
> Important to More Important.
> - Now in each of the quadrants 1, 2, 3 and 4,
> write down everything on your To-Do list,
> placing each item into one of the four
> quadrants.
> - In quadrant 1, write each task that is both very
> important and very urgent.
> - Continue to quadrant 2, writing the rest of
> your very important but less urgent tasks.
> - Then write your less important tasks in
> quadrants 3 and 4 depending upon their
> urgency.

Guess what? You've just defined your priority 1, 2, 3,
and 4 tasks. It should go without saying that you should
work on them in that order. Urgent things that are
unimportant will cease to steal time from things that are
more important. Soon you'll find that you have fewer
fires to put out because you are applying your time
more optimally, doing the things that really matter first.

OK now that you've got things prioritized, let's form
that startup you're dying to work on.

16

CHAPTER 2 - FORMATION

"We go in with eyes wide open and recognize there will be a lot of hard work involved. But we anticipate having success. We feel like we have assembled a great group of people."
- Troy Aikman, pro and college football Hall of Famer

To form your new business you'll need a team, a product or service idea, a business model and a value proposition. Let's start with the team. Why? Because the team's more important than your idea.

Co-founders

Who is going to execute the steps necessary to build your business? You and your co-founders. Your idea may be inspired, but inspiration without execution is a recipe for tragedy. You will need someone who can sell, someone who knows the market, and someone who can write code. These three roles are required.

- The Salesperson
- The Domain Expert
- The Technologist

If you have one or two people that can fulfill all three roles then it's possible to start with a team of one or two. But I recommend one person for each of these roles because there is going to be so much to do and it's great to have people with whom to collaborate, share the workload and provide encouragement. Your chances of success are much greater if you don't try to go it alone.

How do you find co-founders? They might be people you already know: college buddies, co-workers, former co-workers or friends. They need to be local unless you're thinking of moving to them[7]. Start with your

---

[7] Virtual companies (where there is no physical location and people can live anywhere) can work. In fact I'm on the Board of a startup right now that has no office. Everyone works from home and their homes are in separate cities. This style is more and more popular and grew out of the telecommuting trend that began late in the last century. But I don't recommend this for a startup because distance gets in the way of starting fast. It's fine to work from home, but you should be able to get together with your co-founders easily and often.

network and see who's interested, willing and available to co-found (not *confound!*) the business with you.

> **Find Co-founders**: If you've exhausted your personal network and still need to fill a role, there are lots of places to meet co-founders. Go to your local Tech Meetup (**www.meetup.com**) and talk to the people that show up to the meeting. Attend a hackathon (google it). Contact local colleges, universities and Chambers of Commerce and talk to the people in their entrepreneurship programs. Find out if your town has a tech business incubator or entrepreneur's roundtable and go talk to people there. Generally people like to act as match-makers, so you'll quickly get introduced to a number of potential co-founders.

A word of advice – when talking with potential co-founders, drop the gnarly lingo, dude. Seriously…don't use words like "rockstar", "guru", "ninja", or any others of that ilk that may come along. These metaphors are so overused that they have become meaningless. If you actually had to articulate in plain language what you mean when you say "guru ninja", what would that be[8]? Strive to be clear and it will save you both time and headaches later on.

---

[8] Is a ninja someone who can slice through a problem while remaining silent and unseen? Is a guru someone who can effectively coach others?

My advice is to choose co-founders with whom you are truly excited to be working. Don't just fill a role with the first warm body that is willing to take it. Use the following descriptions to help decide the most appropriate additions to your team.

The Salesperson

The Salesperson is a person who can meet a stranger and within five minutes get their business card and an appointment for a follow-up meeting. It's obvious why you need this role filled. More startups fail due to having too few paying customers than for any other reason. The Salesperson is naturally predisposed to listen to and be interested in learning about your customers, their requirements and their objections. But it's not just customers that you need. You need partners, investors and other people to help you build your business. The Salesperson's talents and people skills will be invaluable in these areas as well.

The Domain Expert

The Domain Expert understands the market you're targeting. He or she knows the language and jargon of the industry you're serving. For example, if your market is NASCAR fans, the domain expert will know a lot about racing, cars, drivers, teams and how the circuit works. The Domain Expert can help identify real problems that your product or service can address, may have contacts that can become early customers and can go with the Salesperson to add credibility to meetings.

The Technologist

Somebody has to build the prototype of your product or service. The technical co-founder should know CSS3, HTML5, LAMP (Linux, Apache, MySQL, PHP), and AJAX (Asynchronous JavaScript and XML) and be able to integrate open-source libraries to build your product prototype. Basically he or she should know how to code.

> Unless you've already found your tech person, I recommend that you go to **findthetechguy.com** and read every section. This will not only give you ideas on where to look, but more importantly it will help you understand what you're looking for and avoid common missteps. After that, you can go to a Tech Meetup or online forum like **techco-founder.com**.

What if you're just not able to find someone for one of these roles? I suggest that you don't wait. Start fast and keep looking. You will find the right partners and co-founders soon enough. I don't recommend outsourcing development to contractors at this stage.

Don't worry too much about bookkeeping, accounting, and legal skills. If one of you has these skills, great. If not, you can easily get the help you need from professionals for a fee.

Your Product or Service

A lot of entrepreneurs start with an idea like, "wouldn't it be great if…" Having an idea is fine, but how do you know if your idea is any good? Here are some tests you can perform to determine if your idea is good enough to begin with. Don't worry if it's not perfect. You'll be adjusting all the time in response to customer feedback, if not throwing out the original ideal and moving in a different direction. Startups are expected to pivot until a scalable repeatable business is found. But even so, your basic idea of your product or service has to pass the following three criteria:

1. Does your idea solve a real problem for an easily identifiable group of people (your market)? By real problems, I mean something that is a pain or at least an annoyance. Ask people in your market about the problem you're solving and see how much of a priority it would be for them if you could solve it. How much do your prospective customers care about what you're doing?

2. Do you know of any competitors for your solution? If you answer, "No" to this one you should be worried. If there is no competition for your idea, chances are, there is no market either. Try asking the question a different way. How do people solve the problem now? The answer will point you to your competition. If there are still no competitors, it may be that you are too early – that the market is not yet ready

for your solution. Unfortunately, being early is the same as being wrong[9].

3. Conversely, if there are competitors then there is a market. But can you say what's better about your solution for a particular segment of that market? Always have in mind the point or points that make you unique.

> Talk to prospects about your product or service. Write down your answers to the above three questions as well as the feedback you get from prospects and talk about the answers with your co-founders. Are you on to something or not?

---

[9] The first company I co-founded, Coherent Research, Inc. manufactured a Content Addressable Memory (CAM) chip my team and I conceived while in graduate school. We had the most advanced CAM on the market and I spent a lot of my time evangelizing the product with various potential customers. Cypress Semiconductor licensed the CAM architecture for $750,000 advance plus royalties for five years, but then reneged on the contract and never manufactured the product in volume. Years later with the expansion of the Internet the market for CAM chips took off and today they are used in every high-performance Internet and Ethernet router on the planet (millions of units). If we had licensed our chip roughly three years later, we might have received millions of dollars in royalties or perhaps would have been acquired for mid eight figures. We were right about CAM, but we were early for the market. It was the same as being wrong.

The Business Model[10]

Simply put, the business model is how you plan to make money. For software, web and mobile applications there are choices of business model that must be made – software as a service (SaaS) or licensed, freemium[11] or advertising-supported, pay-per-use or monthly subscription?

This is the heart of the struggle for every startup, particularly in the web space. If you can dream it you can build it but you'll spend a lot of time trying to figure out how to make money. Some of the biggest web companies scaled without having an explicit business model (e.g. Facebook and Twitter) but they are the exception. Investors will buy in if they see massive customer adoption, particularly in the consumer internet space. Otherwise, you need to make money.

Your business model should be a match with how your target market wants to buy. Sometimes your

---

[10] Academics use the phrase business model differently than I do here. When you have time, it's well worth reading Osterwalder's *Business Model Generation*, which defines a company's business model fully.

[11] Give away a basic version of the product or service; charge for the premium version.

opportunity comes primarily from your innovative business model rather than from new technology[12].

I have trouble taking a startup team seriously if they tell me, "I don't know," when I ask them how they make money. You always need an answer to this question even if it changes from time to time. It doesn't have to be the perfect answer as you will be testing and adapting as you learn more about your market.

Differentiation

It's important to know exactly how your product or service is unique and how you are different from your competition. But differences alone are not enough – they have to bring additional value to the customer in order to be considered a competitive differentiator. Of course value is as perceived by the customer so it is not always obvious and certainly not fixed. Your customers' perception of value can change with fashion, trends, fads and even advertising. But value is always determined by how well a product or service fulfills a customer's need. Generally we think of solving problems, providing convenience or helping the

---

[12] For example, when Salesforce.com was introduced to the market, it was arguably no better than other sales force automation products. The Software as a Service business model helped salesforce defeat its competitors more effectively than any new technology.

customer avoid a pain. No doubt these are valuable things.

Human needs have been defined more broadly by Maslow's hierarchy of needs[13], and the perceived value of a product or service can be very powerfully influenced by all levels of this hierarchy.

Maslow's Hierarchy of Needs

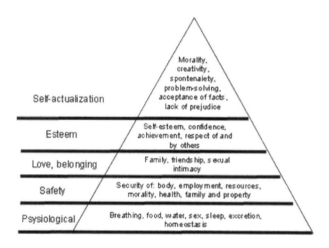

Identifying which basic human needs are satisfied by your product or service will give you insight and ideas for how you can differentiate yourself from your competition. For example, before the Apple iPod, no

---

[13] Defined by Abraham Maslow in his 1943 paper *A Theory of Human Motivation*. I also recommend reading *Maslow on Management*, which is a great book for an aspiring CEO.

one knew they needed 1,000 songs in their pocket. Owning the iPod might engender a sense of belonging and self-esteem in some people (the second highest tier in the hierarchy). In others, buying songs in the iTunes store rather than pirating them appeals to their sense of morality (the highest level in the hierarchy). As long as a customer's needs on lower tiers are met, their motivation moves to the higher tiers. The higher the tier, the stronger the motivation.

> Make a list of the human needs that your product or service fulfills. Be specific. See if you can identify at least one need potentially fulfilled by your product or service from each level of the hierarchy.

To continue with the example of the iPod, it is obvious that a great deal of attention went into designing the user experience. But the user experience is not just defined by the software and hardware. It is defined by the sum total of all interactions a user has with your company, including your product or service.

There are three possible dimensions across which you can differentiate the user experience your company delivers from that of your competition

- technical innovation,
- operational excellence, or
- customer intimacy.

Together these three dimensions create the complete customer or user experience.

Differentiation Chart

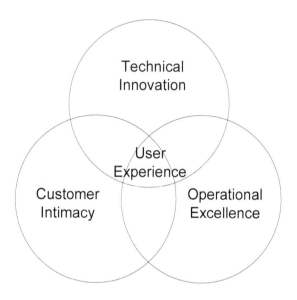

Technical Innovation has to do with features and benefits of your product or service. That is anything you can do better than your competitors by applying your technology. Most tech startups focus exclusively on this dimension, so it shouldn't be hard to list how your product or service is better in this regard. For example, perhaps your product brings high definition video to an online service where your competition only offers standard definition. However, the most powerful use of technology is often to make a product simpler and easier to use[14].

Operational Excellence has to do with the value of how you deliver your product or service. Is it easy to order? Was it delivered efficiently and on time? How reliable is it in operation? Does the product or service perform consistently and predictably or is it a "crap shoot?" How easily can customers get their questions answered and problems resolved? How accurate is your billing? How efficiently does the company resolve any dispute? How important do you think your product or service's technical innovation is to a customer if you can't give the right answers to these questions? Even if you get everything else right, a major flaw in your operations can bring down the entire business.

"Your expected hold time is 63 minutes"

---

[14] Steleus invented an ingeniously simple software product called SMS Welcome which sends a text message like "Welcome to Orange UK" to mobile phone users when they enter a country. This feature increased our customers' roaming revenues by 22%. Sophisticated features added later didn't improve this much.

<u>Customer Intimacy</u> is not about how well you know your customers, but rather how well your customers feel you understand their needs. Do they feel as though your company is a trusted advisor or friend? Do you have specific domain expertise that they value? Do you have a relationship with your customers? In specific vertical markets you may be able to defeat a larger competitor by knowing your customers' business better[15].

Notice that I left out price. Price is not a differentiator. If your products or services are differentiated, you can charge a premium price without any loss of market share. If your product or service is not differentiated, then it is a commodity and the lowest priced competitor will prevail in the market. Since your company is a startup you can not survive for long competing solely on price because you will run out of cash before your competition does.

Most companies tend to focus on one primary dimension of differentiation. Great companies exceed expectations in all three dimensions. For example,

---

[15] When I was Chief Marketing Officer at PacketExchange we offered technically superior services at lower prices but could not displace our competitor Sohonet in providing data network services to the film industry. Sohonet understands its customers well and goes out of its way to cater to their needs. Customer intimacy allows Sohonet to maintain a healthy business and win against much larger competitors.

Apple regularly creates technically innovative new products, their operational excellence is generally superb and they maximize customer intimacy through offering one on one training and problem solving in their retail stores. At the minimum, your startup needs to have a way to beat your competition in one dimension, and you also must be good enough (by the customer's definition) in the other two.

> List your differentiators: draw a differentiation chart like the one above. List in each circle the ways in which your company, product or service will bring more value to customers when they compare you to your competition.

Value Proposition

Your value proposition is a few sentences that summarize the answers to two crucial questions from your customer's point of view, "What's in it for me?" and "Why should I buy from you?" The answer to the first question is your value to the customer. The answer to the second question is your differentiation from your competitors.

As always, don't agonize too long over this, as you'll be adapting your value proposition in response to feedback from customers. Just make sure that you've always got a value proposition, that you can articulate it comfortably and succinctly and that it matches the best and most current feedback that you've gotten from the market.

What's in it for me?

Customers buy products and services to solve problems that arise during their day-to-day life. So your product or service must match a circumstance that customers find themselves in. How does it make their lives easier? I recommend that you stay away from the three words, "faster, better, cheaper" if at all possible. Rather focus on "simpler" or "easier." For example, the Apple voice assistant application, Siri, makes it easier (not to mention safer!) to use your iPhone for calls and texts while driving. This is part of the *value* of the iPhone 4s to a *market* (i.e. people who need to stay in contact while driving).

Improve or Disrupt?

"Why should I buy from you?" is another way of asking, "What makes you and your product or service unique?" The kind of differentiation you have from your competitors has a great deal to do with your strategy. Is your product an improvement or a disruption?

Targeting your competitors existing customers with a better product (improvement) encourages your competition to try to beat you. If you do not succeed quickly enough, the competitors in the market will simply destroy you. Entrenched competitors have tremendous advantages over startups once they decide (or you prove) that the market values the improvements you've made. Why? Because they already have the customers and can out-spend you many times over on marketing and development. Your competitors want to retain their current customers and will defend that position against you.

If you start fast and grow fast, you may catch your competitor unaware and win some market share. Your competitor may decide to acquire your company as the most efficient way to recapture the position you occupy. But there is also the risk that your competition will choose to block and/or crush you.

The other approach is to disrupt the market. You can do this by looking for customers that your competition can't serve, or for some reason doesn't want or care about. For example, you can target customers on the low-end of your competitor's market that they are actually happy to lose. Or target non-customers who will welcome a simple product that serves their needs. Since this market is not buying from your competition, there is less likelihood that your competition will fight you for them. Later, as you gain market share, your innovation may end up destroying your competition[16].

---

[16] When Google was founded in 1998, they had a better web search engine than Alta Vista. Within a year they decided that their

Prove it!

Last but not least, your value proposition should have proof points. How do I know what you say is true? Give me examples. Real customer stories and feedback are much more compelling than your opinion. As a rule of thumb, have at least two proof points for every claim you make in your value proposition.

> **Write down your Value Proposition**: Include differentiation and proof points. For example hypothetical company, YoYoTech might say, "YoYoTech solves the problem of video review and approval for advertising agencies. Unlike Vimeo, YouTube, or other online video platforms, YoYoTech keeps the data private and secure without sacrificing ease of use. The BIG agency found that using YoYoTech saved them an average of $1,000 per campaign over their old method of shipping DVDs to clients. Their clients are also delighted to be able to give direct feedback online."

---

business model was to attract pay-per-click advertising dollars based on what the user was searching for. At the time, most advertising was done in conventional media (print, TV, radio). Major media outlets and advertising companies weren't very interested in online advertising. Today Google's revenues are 90% from advertising and they take billions of dollars a year from their conventional competition, in the process forcing them to adapt or be destroyed.

Elevator Pitch

You've no doubt heard the story that engendered the term Elevator Pitch. You find yourself in an elevator with your ideal customer or investor and you have just 30 seconds to make the pitch that will change your life. It's not just elevators that come into play here. It turns out that it's human nature to take a first impression from each person you meet. Everyone is overworked and on information overload so how do you make yourself relevant to them in that crucial first 30 seconds? How do you avoid the future regret of having missed (or blown) that opportunity? By preparing thoroughly for that event ahead of time.

> **Craft an Elevator Pitch**: Translate your value proposition into a story that illustrates what you do for people. Someone faces tragedy if they don't solve their problem. Then say very simply, with no jargon or technical words, how your product or service solves that problem. Use strong verbs and images to make your story memorable. Come up with a couple of variations for different audiences.

Your goal is to get the listener interested. Don't ask for the order or referral during the elevator pitch. Just ask for more time, either an appointment or a call and try to get the person's contact information. If they are truly interested, they'll give it to you. If not, you've saved them and yourself wasted time by being brief. Either way, give them your card. They might think of someone to refer to you later.

Write down your elevator pitch down. Pitch to yourself in the mirror. Practice using the voice memo recorder on your iPhone or Droid. Listen to yourself. Time it; make sure it's under 30 seconds. Practice on your mentors, friends and family. Ask for feedback. What did they take away from the pitch?

Continually improve both the wording and your delivery. You will use this compact form of your value proposition at trade shows, at Meetups, on social media, in bars, at family gatherings, and yes, in elevators!

Cash Flow

> *"If I had eight hours to chop down a tree, I'd spend six sharpening my axe."*
> *- Abraham Lincoln*

You don't need an MBA degree to start a company because a startup isn't a smaller version of a large company – it's completely different. Nonetheless a startup is a business and there are things you simply must manage. If you've managed a business before or attended business school, chances are that you already know the basics. If you're a technical co-founder, you may not. Either way, knowing which tools you need is not enough. You have to use them regularly and diligently to avoid fatal mistakes and keep focused on what's important to survive as a business.

The quickest and surest way to kill a business is to run out of cash. Sometimes it's inevitable, but when it can be avoided and isn't, it's a tragedy[17]. Maintaining a clear understanding of cash flow at all times is necessary and a cash flow forecast is a basic prerequisite for the job.

I recommend that all startups have a monthly cash flow forecast (as in the example diagram). By constantly updating the cash flow forecast you will know when in the future you're likely to run low so you will be able to make plans to avoid running out. Cash flow forecasting is all about timing and contingency planning. You need to understand where your cash is coming from and what might delay its arrival. This becomes more complex and more critical as the business grows because as the numbers grow larger, unpredicted swings have a greater potential impact. Cash comes in as customers or partners pay you, as you borrow money, as investors write you checks and as vendors credit you

---

[17] You'd be surprised how often a startup CEO surprises his investors with the news, "If you don't put more money into the company right away, we will be out of cash and won't make payroll next month." Understandably this often leads to the CEO being replaced, especially if it appears to have been avoidable. Even if you don't have investors yet, get in the habit of always knowing your cash position.

for returns. If you invoice a customer how soon will they pay you? You need each contract to specify clear payment terms[18]. What if your customer *ages your invoice*[19]? Predicting correctly the date cash will come in is one of the subtle arts of running a business.

Cash Flow Forecast Spreadsheet

	Jan	Feb	Mar	Apr	May	Jun	Jul	Aug	Sep	Oct	Nov	Dec
Starting Cash												
Sources												
Total												
Uses												
Total												
Ending Cash												

[18] For example, Net 30 terms means that they have 30 days from receiving your invoice to pay you.

[19] Some customers wire payment as soon as I invoice them. Others send a check after months of delay. Guess which customers I value more highly. Companies that manage their cash flow by "aging accounts payable" are borrowing money from you without your permission. You should talk with slow-paying customers and consider letting them go if they don't abide by contracted payment terms.

> **Create a Cashflow Forecast**: Make a spreadsheet in Numbers, Excel, or Google Docs to match the one pictured above.
> - Start with the current month and next to *Starting Cash*, put your company's bank balance.
> - Put in line by line everything you know about future payments to be made under *Uses* of cash. Total these under each month.
> - List every payment that you expect to receive in the appropriate month under Sources of cash. Total these under each month.
> - *Ending Cash* is calculated by adding each month's total under *Sources* to each month's *Starting Cash* and subtracting that month's total under *Uses*.
> - Copy each month's *Ending Cash* into the place for *Starting Cash* for the following month.
> - Keep this forecast up to date, modifying it every time you receive or make a payment and every time you learn something new about the timing of receipts or payments.

I like to set up the row called Ending Cash so that any negative number will show up in red. Once you've populated your forecast with everything you know, you can quickly scan the columns and figure out how much runway you have. The first time that Ending Cash turns red, you're out of cash (and unless you do something about it, you're out of business).

If Ending Cash is in the red, your choices are simple: find more or accelerate payments from sources of cash, delay some uses of cash or raise money from investors.

The cash flow forecast tells you when, how much and for what the investment money will be used. Keep your cashflow forecast up to date. This tool will not only help you plan, it will actually help you sleep better at night because instead of worrying unnecessarily you'll know exactly what's going on.

So now you have a startup company with a team, a product or service, a business model and a value proposition. You know where your cash is coming from and where it's going. Now what? On to the next stage, Prototype!

CHAPTER 3 - PROTOTYPE

"Get your prototype out there as soon as you can. Don't spend six months releasing your first prototype. It's going to fall flat. Instead, get a prototype into the hands of your potential customers as soon as you can. You need to learn as quickly as possible what's wrong with the idea so you can fix it."
- Vinicius Vacanti, blogger and co-founder of Yipit

How do you know if you're right? You've already talked to everyone who'll listen about your startup and incorporated their feedback into your plans. Now it's time to prototype your product or service and let customers try it out. You'll need to create a landing page, collect prospects, prototype your product, get users signed up and get feedback from these early adopters who will test drive your product or service. Here are the steps to start this process fast.

Create a landing page

The purpose of the landing page is to collect email addresses from visitors. Tell the visitor very clearly what problem your product or service will solve for them (remember your value proposition?). Offer the visitor early access to your prototype in return for their email address. Include a value statement - a really simple phrase that gets the point of your product or service across.

> **Create your landing page today:** Pick a domain name. You can check to see if it's available and buy it on godaddy.com, or another domain name registrar. Don't spend too much time picking one. You can change it later if you want to. Don't spend money on a "vanity" domain name now.
>
> You can create a landing page anyway you want, but here are three easy ways that require no programming:
> 1. Use Wordpress.com to create the page (free +$12/year to map your domain name) and integrate it with a plug-in like getPremise.com ($85).
> 2. Use Unbounce.com ($25+/month after 30-day free trial)
> 3. Use LaunchRock.com (free).

Examples of simple value statements:

- Foursquare: "Make the Real World Easier to Use"
- Tumblr: "The Easiest Way To Blog"
- Yelp: "Real People. Real Reviews"
- Soundhound: "Instant Music Search and Discovery"
- eVoice: "A radically better phone number"

Collect Prospects' Email Addresses

The email addresses you collect comprise your prospect list. These people will become your early users. When your prototype is ready, you'll email a portion of these users and get them to test-drive your product or service. You'll make changes to the prototype in response to their feedback, invite more users from your list and continue the process until the prototype works well. This early feedback will give you the opportunity to make changes that otherwise might have caused your company to fail if you hadn't known to make them until later.

In order to get these email addresses, you need to get people to visit your landing page and sign up there. Do not send unsolicited emails (spam) to your prospects. It's not just a much-hated practice, spam violates network policies and in some jurisdictions, the law. Get users to sign up; it's not spam if you have their authorization.

> ## Get people to visit your landing page:
> - Include your value statement and link to your landing page in your email signature.
> - Add the link to all your profiles on LinkedIn, Facebook, Twitter and every other account you have.
> - Print a business card with your value statement and link on it and hand it out everywhere you go, even to people you know. Your local copy shop can do this for you while you wait for about $20.
> - Facebook Ads and Google Ads can drive traffic to your site if you pick the right keywords and demographics. It's worth $50-100 if you spend it carefully.
> - When people visit your page, offer them something to tweet it out to their friends and put the buttons to do so right on the page.
> - Ask your friends and mentors (especially connectors[20]) to retweet your message.

Now that you've got people visiting your landing page, how do you get them to give up their email address? When someone goes to your landing page and fills in the form it is called a Conversion. The ratio of people who fill out the form to total visitors is called the Conversion Rate. Obviously you want to maximize

---

[20] Connectors are people who know and influence an unusual number of other people. Read Malcolm Gladwell's *The Tipping Point* if you want to understand this phenomenon in detail.

your conversion rate. Here are 11 suggestions to help you do that:

1. Use active verbs in your value statement like "register", "join", "get", "own", "feel", "have", "know", "boost", "love". Avoid more passive words like "submit", "imagine", "flow", "read".

2. Include a phone number on your landing page. Simply putting a contact phone number on the page adds credibility to your business and gives comfort to your users. You don't have to use your personal home or mobile number. Check out evoice.com where you can get a toll-free or local number free for six months.

3. Ask for the minimum information you need. The easier the sign-up process, the more likely people are to do it. If all you ask for is an email address, you'll get a much higher conversion rate than if you require full name and phone number. Zip / postal codes are also pretty innocuous and can be very helpful in terms of locating your contacts. You can get more information later when you are better known and have established a level of trust. Do ask for what you need though.

4. Make the form easy to find. Make sure the form is "above the fold[21]" and that the submit button

---

[21] "Above the Fold" means the part of your landing page that appears on screen, without scrolling, when you first navigate to the site.

is large and colorful. If you have multiple pages in your website, then put the form on every page (in a sidebar).

5. Offer them something. For example, you're offering them early access to your prototype. Other ideas are 30 days free service or a chance to win an iPad. Be creative.

6. Create a demo video and post it on your landing page. It doesn't matter whether it's a live action demo, animated demo or something else. Video increases conversion rates because it answers the visitors questions without requiring them to do anything.

7. Use testimonials as soon as you have some. These work better if you can quote a real person and perhaps even put their picture up.

8. Make your site layout interesting and eye-catching and create a catch-all so that your site doesn't give 404 errors if someone tries to go to the wrong place.

9. Try multiple versions of your landing page to see which one works the best (gives the most conversions). You can experiment with colors, placement of items, product image size and forms. You can test formal versus informal versus edgy language. Find out what works best for your specific audience. Many tools support this testing such as Google's Website Optimizer and Analytics.

10. Create a simple privacy policy and abide by it. If you say, "We will never share your email

address or other information with any third party," it inspires confidence.

11. <u>Instill a sense of urgency</u> by using deadlines like "before December 31," and a sense of exclusivity such as, "Only registered members will be invited to the launch party."

Above all, play fair with people that register on your site. Give the prizes that you promise, respect and abide by your stated privacy policy, and don't ever surprise them. Customers hate surprises (remember Netflix' attempt to raise prices?).

Managing your list of prospects is important too. You can use an excel spreadsheet, a mailing list program like MailChimp or a Customer Relationship Management (CRM) product like Salesforce.com or Sugar CRM. The costs and capabilities vary widely. I like a combination of MailChimp and Salesforce.com because you can start out for $5/user/month and keep a record of every interaction you have with a prospect. Later you can upgrade as you need more powerful CRM features. At this stage, keep it as simple and cheap as possible but get the capabilities you absolutely need.

Prototype your product or service

Now is the time to see if your value proposition is correct. Does your product solve a real problem that a real group of people experience in real life? You think it does, and everyone you've talked to thinks it does. Well let's test that. While you are setting up your landing page and getting the word out, your technical team member(s) should be building a working prototype of your product. I recommend that you develop as much in-house as you can so that you can easily make changes. Your prototype should be a Minimum Viable Product

Minimum Viable Product

You don't want to waste time or money finding out if your product or service solves a real problem and fits a real market. That is why you design the Minimum Viable Product (MVP)[22]. In order to start fast, you need to *take features out* of your product. "What?!" you say, "Take features out? Don't I want to add as many features as possible?" No.

Write down a list of everything your product is supposed to do. Then start eliminating functions which aren't absolutely necessary to fulfill your value proposition. Don't make the mistake of adding every feature that any prospect asks for. That will just add to the cost and time required to do the prototype. There will be time to add features later, once you've found a market that is interested in your value proposition.

---

[22] There are some great books on this process. If you're interested to learn more, read *The Lean Startup*, by Eric Ries, *Four Steps to the Epiphany*, by Steve Blank and *The Entrepreneur's Guide to Customer Development*, by Brant Cooper and Patrick Vlaskovits.

Your MVP should have only those features that allow the product to be deployed, and no more. You can hand-select from your prospect list those early adopters to whom you will give access to your prototype MVP. This subset needs to be forgiving of bugs, interested enough to give feedback, and capable of benefiting from the vision of which your prototype is an early instance.

The whole point is to start fast and avoid wasting time and money building products that customers do not want. The purpose of the MVP is to maximize the information you learn about the customer's real needs with the least effort, money and time expended.

In the next stage, you'll be iterating the process of making changes and getting feedback. The faster you can complete an iteration, the better chance you have of finding a scalable business model and a product that fits a market need.

Wireframe

You can design the basic flow of your product/service using a wireframe, which is basically a sketch of what your pages will look like, where you will place buttons and information on the screen and how one screen flows into another. Tools like Balsamiq Mockups (balsamiq.com, $79) or iMockups ($6.99 in the iTunes store) are great for this purpose. While I've seen wireframes done in Keynote, Powerpoint or on a cocktail napkin, I strongly recommend using an automated tool for your wireframe as it will make it much easier for you and your co-founders to visualize the flow of the pages that you're looking to build.

Coding

If you've not attracted a technical co-founder yet, take your mockup with you to tech meetups, hackathons and startup weekends, show it off and see if you can change your destiny. Web developers are not as hard to find as people would have you believe. They are just bombarded by wannabe's who haven't thought things through. If you've followed the steps I've outlined so far, you'll be way ahead of the crowd. After all, you're already known in these circles from your previous recruiting activities. Your progress and staying power will make a very good impression. You will probably be able to attract a CTO-to-be.

If not you still have two options: 1) outsource the prototype development to a freelancer or professional dev shop or 2) become technical enough to do the first prototype yourself. Only you can make the choice, but I'd encourage you to try 2). The tradeoffs are obvious.

If you choose 1), you'll spend a chunk of cash even though you still don't know how well your product fits a market. You have the additional problem of making sure that the outsourced programmer(s) develops the right prototype. This is less trivial than it sounds to the uninitiated. The upside is that you will get your prototype built and out there fast.

If you choose 2) then the time it takes to develop the prototype will depend upon how quickly you can learn. Start with HTML5 and CSS3. There are excellent resources online (like codelesson.com), books and courses which can help. Don't be daunted by this. Just dive in and start finding out what you need to know[23].

Remember, it's only temporary. Once you get some users and they refer their friends, before you know it you'll have some market validation. The farther you get, the more likely that great technical co-founders will come looking for you.

When developing your prototype keep in mind the following:

- You're developing a Minimum Viable Product (MVP). You don't want to build a complete product, just the core functionality that demonstrates your value proposition. Depending upon what you're doing this may take anywhere from a day to a week for an experienced developer. If you're learning

---

[23] For a start, take a look at 20thingsilearned.com. Don't be put off by the kiddie-book graphics. You need to know everything that's in here before you go any further.

as you go, give yourself a break and take as much time as you need.

- Spend most of the time on the user experience – make it small, easy, simple and wicked cool. This is one of the reasons you spent time on your wireframe.

- Use open source apps, plug-ins and frameworks. You can find just about any function you need already developed, available for free and including the source code. Check out Jquery and Django. The possibilities are nearly endless. You can change your mind later and replace code as needed. Just get something to work and get it out there.

- If you run into a bug, search it on Google or stackoverflow.com. Somebody has probably already solved the problem. Reach out to the in-person developer community at meet-ups in your area too. People love to feel smarter than you by helping you solve your problem.

- Don't try to make your prototype perfect. Do enough testing to make sure it's not super annoying for users and then get it out there.

Release the tiger! (I mean prototype)

When you think you're ready, move your prototype from the development area to the production area of your web server and make sure it's still working. Select the best prospects from your list. If you can, limit the initial set to your local area. Give them login credentials or simply point them to the application's web page and ask them to:

1. Use the prototype,
2. Invite their friends to register,
3. Give you feedback.

Keep track of which users actually create accounts and which ones ignore your email and never log-in or use your site. Since you will only have a few users at this stage, you can afford to treat them really well. Send them a survey to find out what they like and don't like. After a week or so, throw them a party at a local restaurant or bar. Ask them to bring friends. Bring your friends. You don't have to spend a lot of money – you can even have a cash bar. Just getting people together is going to help build community. Tell your users that you appreciate them. Blog about the party, the feedback you're getting, about how much you appreciate your users.

If you've reached this point, you're ready for the next stage: Promote, Validate, Adjust and Iterate your product or service and business model.

What if you aren't getting traction?

> *"Every startup goes from failure to failure until it finds success"*
> *- Steve Blank, serial entrepreneur, author, professor*

After I got my BS degree, I lived briefly in the DC area where it snows only rarely. That winter, two inches of snow fell and quickly turned to ice on the unplowed, unsalted roads. Soon every on/off ramp was blocked by someone standing on the gas pedal going nowhere fast.

Don't be that guy. If you're not getting traction, stop, think, and figure out what to do next.

We just need more cash!

Very, very few startups get it right in one. There are lots of reasons your idea may not be getting traction. It's possible that your idea is a no-go. Take a look at the kind of feedback you're getting: interest or disinterest? Ask people why and you'll get clues to what you need to change. Maybe you need to revisit some of the earlier steps with a different approach.

1. Maybe you need to try a different market segment or even a different market altogether, especially if you don't have passionate early evangelists for your product or service.

2. If you have loyal fans (just not enough) you might try a different price (higher or lower), a different way of charging (e.g. per transaction vs monthly), a different model (e.g. change from charging to ad supported).

Don't lose heart. One reason for starting fast is so that you can fail fast and still have time, money, and energy to try again. Have a rational conversation with your co-founders about what the market is telling you. Go over where you've lost and probe why. Constantly share what you've learned with your co-founders and figure out what you should try next.

You've already gained experience by going through the steps in the process and learning to use the tools. By now you have met a lot of people who will be helpful to you on your next iteration. The key is that you did not scale prematurely. You only used some of your prospects. Your next attempt will be easier and faster than the previous time around.

I don't know a single successful entrepreneur who hasn't failed before they've succeeded. It's one of the main ways we learn.

If it's time to pivot[24], you may need input from some mentors. Remember all those meetings you attended when you were putting your team together? You probably ran into some serial entrepreneurs (people who had done it before). The great thing about serial entrepreneurs is that they've probably had both wins and fails in their past experience. Guess what? Both are rich learning experiences. A serial entrepreneur is just the right mentor for you at this stage.

<u>Reach out to a couple of serial entrepreneurs</u>: and ask them if they'll meet you and your team for a mentoring session. Tell them everything – what your assumptions were, what you did to test them, what you think you should do next. Really listen and don't answer the feedback. Just take notes and don't decide what to do until you've had input from a couple of mentors. Then make your own decision. Remember to trust data over opinion every time.

A mentor is someone who helps you for the satisfaction of doing so, whereas a consultant is someone who gets paid for helping.

---

[24] A quick change of direction. A pivot can be any substantial change in choice of idea, target market, pricing strategy, channel to market, etc.

CHAPTER 4 – ITERATE[25]

"Your idea isn't the real value, it's you. The value lies in your ability to learn from potential customers [and] iterate based on those learnings. Those iterations will determine whether or not your startup will be successful, not the initial idea."
- Vinicius Vacanti

You've built a prototype and you've gotten a few (or a few hundred) users to sign up. The next step is to ramp things up a bit, with the goal of finding and validating

---

[25] "**Iteration** means the act of repeating a process usually with the aim of approaching a desired goal or target or result. Each repetition of the process is also called an "iteration," and the results of one iteration are used as the starting point for the next iteration." - Wikipedia

the right fit between your market and your product/service and business model. It's not time yet to scale the business! In fact, doing so now could cost you dearly. You don't need to raise a big round of capital, you don't need to hire more employees, and you don't need a big office with a salary to match. Wait for it.

However, you do need more users than in the Prototype stage. How many? That depends upon your specific product or service, but think in terms of at least 100 and possibly as many as a few thousand users, but not so many that you need to build out a lot of infrastructure. Unless you've been very lucky and already have a lot of users, you'll need to do some additional promotion. This might be a good time to define which customers you really want.

Ideal Customer

Your *Ideal Customer* is not an actual, real-life customer, but rather a model you can use to help you focus your time on prospects with a good fit to your offering. This model of the perfect customer you'd like to have will change over time as you get feedback from the market and adapt to it. When you pivot, your Ideal Customer will change.

Who is the perfect person or company to buy your product or service? Where are they located geographically? How large a company do they work for? What are their preferences? What is their income level? Be as specific as you can be.

Define your Ideal Customer:

- List best and worst users with whom you've done business (just customers, not prospects).
- The best will include those that have spent the most money, given you the best exposure (e.g. told their friends, tweeted or written positive things about you) and given you the least trouble (e.g. complaints, support calls, custom feature or refund requests).
- The worst are users you wish you hadn't signed.
- Now list the characteristics of the best and worst customers for example:
• Industry vertical (e.g. advertising, automotive…)
• Geographic location
• Size of company
• Willingness to pay extra for your differentiators or inflexible on price?
• Fast or slow to make buying decisions?
• Open or secretive and unwilling to cooperate?
• Inside or outside your industry expertise?
- Now write down your model of the Ideal Customer. List the traits of your best customers and then add the opposite of the traits of your worst customers.

Why focus? Because your competition can outspend you, but probably can't out-focus you. Focus on business you can win with your limited resources[26].

If you already have some users, which are the most passionate evangelists for your product or service? Which are the most profitable for you? Find out their traits and you'll have a good start on describing your Ideal Customer.

If you don't know much about your customers, you may need to use a survey. I recommend that you use SurveyMonkey.com to ask your users what their traits are and how satisfied they are with your price, features, service, etc. You can use the results to create a hypothetical model of an Ideal Customer that you can refine as you learn more.

Your Ideal Customer model helps you sort through unlimited sales and marketing opportunities to choose those that are best for your company. Don't chase every potential customer. Put your effort into attracting

---

[26] Steleus built network monitoring software for mobile phone companies. As a small company new to the market we knew that we'd have trouble selling to the largest (e.g. Verizon, AT&T, Sprint), so our ideal customer was the smaller independent companies (e.g. MetroPCS, NTELOS, Leap, Cricket). These were our Ideal Customers. After Tekelec acquired us, with their greater resources we were able to expand into Verizon and the other majors.

more ideal customers. You won't turn down business from less than ideal customers, but you won't spend time and money chasing them.

Target Market

Market segmentation is the process of dividing a market into parts or segments. Your *Target Market* segment is made up of all the potential customers that share the traits of your Ideal Customer. What are the things your best customers have in common? Try to identify traits that will help you find other prospects just like your best customers.

For example, suppose that your best customers are more often than not independent videographers living in Manhattan who prefer using the Apple platform. Your overall market consists of all videographers (independent or otherwise), in all geographies, who work on any video platform. But your target market (for now at least) is much more specific. Focusing on the market segment that has the highest concentration of ideal customers will increase your profitability and your probability of success. You can address the other segments later from a position of greater strength.

Filling in the three variables (e.g. geography, independent or corporate, platform preference) differently defines various market segments. As your business grows, you may be able to expand into adjacent markets (e.g. other geographies, other platforms, corporate) to increase your sales.

Market Segmentation Chart

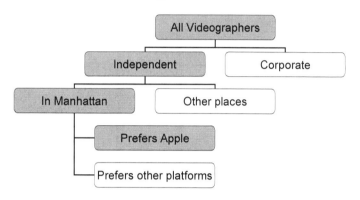

You can determine the size of your target market and other segments by gathering data. You gather primary market data by interacting directly with customers, prospects and influencers. This includes conversations, feedback forms and surveys you send out or create online.

Secondary market data comes from online forums, blogs, magazines and published market research. Be prepared to use primary data to build a bottom-up (specific to general) view of your market by listing the needs of specific customers or prospects and then generalizing. Secondary data can be used in a top-down fashion, taking statistics on the general market and extrapolating more specific estimates for your individual market segments. When the bottom-up and top-down approaches yield roughly the same market sizing, you can have more confidence in your numbers.

Use your Target Market and your model of the Ideal Customer to qualify prospects, decide where and how to advertise, and how to prioritize new feature requests. As you broaden your focus to adjacent segments, prioritize new segments that require the fewest changes to your product or service. Keep track of what's important for each segment you're selling to. When you have to make tradeoffs you'll know who will be affected and how. Whenever you pivot, make sure you repeat the exercise of determining your Ideal Customer and Target Market.

Now that you know which market segment you're targeting and what your ideal customer looks like, it's time to get the word out.

Promote

You've managed to get people to visit your site and some of them to sign up. To scale up by a factor of 10 or so, you can't just do the same things *harder,* you need some different tactics. But first, revisit what you've done and make sure that it's kept pace with your adaptations of your product. Do your website, demo video, and any other promotional material you've got out there still describe what you're doing now? Do they address what your target market cares about? If not, make any adjustments that are necessary to bring them into alignment. Once that's done, you can turn up the volume.

If your solution is a mobile application (app) then it's time to put it in the App Store for your chosen platform(s), iOS and Android. Of course, this alone won't promote your app, as you'll tend to get lost in the hundreds of thousands of other apps there. But it will make it easier for non-technical users to get your app and try it out.

Social Media and Natural Friends

Natural friends are groups of people that should like you and your product. If you haven't already done so, create a Facebook page, a LinkedIn page, a blog and a Twitter feed for your company/product/service. Then search for individuals and groups that attract an audience you're interested in. Join the group, follow the individuals and become an active participant tweeting and commenting regularly. Try to add value; don't just pitch your product.

When you do tweet about your product, spend some time crafting your message to be engaging and clear in less than 140 characters. Make up some funny reasons people would use your app.

Create a YouTube and/or Vimeo channel and post your demo video there. There are large communities of people you can plug into this way. Check out

TubeMogul.com if you want to take your video outreach to another level of sophistication.

Don't forget old-fashioned list-serves/bulletin boards and trade associations. These are great ways to reach people in your market if you're not too salesy in your approach.

Offer promo keys / discount codes to the first 100 members that sign up. Be generous with beta[27] access. These are the people who are going to help promote your business.

Running a contest and inviting users to a launch party are two of my other favorite ways of creating additional buzz. Be creative, but stay within your budget!

Get your iPhone app noticed: Submit a short description of your app to the following influencers. Make sure to follow their submission guidelines: DailyAppShow.Com, AppStoreApps.com, AppCraver.com, 148Apps.com, appsafari.com, iPhoneApps.com, iPhoneApplicationList.com, NativeiPhoneApps.com, iPhoneApps.co.uk, Apptism.com, AppShopper.com or AppRater.com.

---

[27] I use "alpha" to designate a product or service release that you're testing internally and "beta" to mean a release you're testing with people outside the company. Beta users will encounter bugs, so choose a set of the more forgiving ones.

Advertising

Getting results with paid Adwords and Facebook accounts can be difficult, time-consuming and expensive. If you are getting results from the low-budget experiments you did in the last stage, by all means continue and expand your budget somewhat. However, if you haven't cracked the code with paid advertising, then put this technique on the shelf for now. Later you may have the opportunity to hire someone who really knows what they're doing and how to get value for money with these tools.

Generally TV and radio spots are still too expensive at this point. One kind of advertising which is easy to implement and relatively cheap is sponsoring a podcast, vlog, or internet bulletin board. If there are specific groups that you can reach this way, ask the publisher about sponsorship opportunities. For example, you can offer perks to members of Meetup groups. You may be able to get significant exposure within a targeted group for a very reasonable price.

Craigslist is free and popular so put an ad for your solution there. DMOZ.com, the open directory project, is another free resource. Also check out BOTW.com (Best of the Web) which is not free, but still relatively cheap. There may be other sites specific to your target market that could be helpful to you and many offer basic listings for free. For example, in the content space, creativecow.com and behance.net offer a free listing.

Trade Shows

Trade shows can also be an inexpensive way to get the word out if you use a little guerrilla marketing. Check the upcoming tradeshows in your area and see if you can get an "Exhibits Only" pass for free. More and more tradeshows are offering these to increase the perceived booth traffic. Bring your application with you on your phone, tablet or laptop, along with some postcards with a screen shot and your value proposition along with a QR code (two-dimensional bar codes that can be interpreted by a mobile phone camera equipped with a code-reading app) pointing to your web address. As you walk around the tradeshow, ask people if they'd like a free demo or beta access to your solution. People love free stuff. You might pick up a hundred new users in an afternoon if the tradeshow caters to people in your target market.

> **Get a QR code** for your website or app store entry. Websites qrcode.kaywa.com, Qurify.com/en, Delivr.com/qr-code-generator, and Goo.gl will convert a standard URL into a Quick Response (QR) code. Once converted, you can download the QR image file and then attach it to your e-mail signature, upload it as a Facebook profile photo, print it on the back of your business card or post it anywhere you want.

Another way to gain free access to trade shows is by joining a partner in the booth that they're paying for. Have the partner add you to their exhibit staff and you'll get in for free. This has the advantage that you can set up meetings ahead of time and have your prospects meet you at your partner's booth. Friendly tradeshow staff will guide your prospect to your location. And while you're waiting, you can try out your elevator pitch on everyone that comes to the booth. Why would your partner do this for you? Maybe your app utilizes their cloud computing platform, plug-in or framework. So promoting your app promotes their solution too.

You will get invited to trade show parties by other vendors. These are business/social events so it is expected that you're going to tell people about what you do. Go, have a good time and be prepared to hand out your postcards and talk about your app. Be respectful of the fact that the party host is paying for the event and don't disrupt their marketing mission.

Trade association professional meetings and other industry events will often put out requests for volunteers to help out with the meeting. By volunteering some of your time, you'll get to attend the entire conference. Don't pitch during the sessions, as these are purely educational. However, during the breaks and meals, everyone you meet will ask, "What do you do?" That's your cue to tell them how you and your startup are going to change the world and their lives. If they're interested, offer them access and ask them to invite their friends or blog about their experience.

Press

Now that you have a prototype to put in the hands of editors and bloggers, you have a chance to get noticed. Make sure your demo video is up to snuff before you start and that your site is ready for a couple thousand new users. Put up a Press page on your website where anyone can download for free a high-res version of your logo or icon, screen shots, founders' bios, and 50, 100, and 300 word descriptions of your company, value proposition and product or service. You'll be surprised how much traction you get just by making it easy on the media.

So how do you get covered by the bright lights in the blogosphere like TechCrunch, Digg, GigaOm, VentureBeat, Wired, TUAW, New and Noteworthy, LifeHacker or other opinion leaders? Perhaps there are publications that are even more specific to your market that you'd like to get coverage in. Here is how you get your product or service noticed and hopefully written about in someone else's blog:

1. <u>Read the blogs you want to appear in</u> to get an idea what the authors like to write about, their style and how they like to tell a story. Try to understand their worldview.

2. <u>Comment on the blogger's posts</u>. Give some thought to the comments you make and *don't* pitch your product. The idea is to become someone the blogger knows and respects. Believe me, they read your comments. Next start tweeting the blogger's posts out to your network, or use LinkedIn or Facebook if that is more your style. Link to their blog from yours. If you meet socially, spare them your elevator pitch. I know this sounds counterintuitive, but there is a point. You are making deposits in the relationship bank with that blogger. You will earn interest on those deposits later.

3. <u>Draft your own story</u>, to the best of your ability, in your chosen author's voice and style. The better (interesting, engaging, concise) the story, the more likely someone will want to tell it. Make sure there's some drama in the headline, and make sure you are truthful. You could refer to a large company missing the boat ala, "The opportunity Facebook missed," or how fast your company is growing, or the big customer you just won (get their permission first). Tie into trends that your targeted blogger has written about.

4. <u>So what</u>? As you read your story, ask yourself, "So what?" over and over until you've rewritten the story into something that matters or means something. Example: "We're launching a new social gaming site." So what? Get specific. Change that to "Our users are tired of social gaming with bad graphics. We're upgrading the user experience to the level of a

game console so users can really get
immersed."

5. <u>Get rid of all the buzzwords</u> like "killer", "next
big thing", "new new thing" and clichés like
"insanely good," "radically better," and
certainly "the best thing since X." Pop culture
references are OK if they're not too obscure[28].

6. <u>Make comparisons</u>. Most people understand
things more quickly when you can compare
them to something they already know, and tell
them what the differences are. For example,
"MediaCloud is like DropBox for content
professionals. It makes use of distributed cloud
processors to accelerate uploads and
downloads of big media files and takes
advantage of HTML5 to provide a rich set of
tools to view and manipulate all kinds of
graphic and video content."

7. <u>Include a list of your competitors</u> and what
makes you different.

8. <u>Get covered</u>. Once you've done 1-7 above,
there are two ways to get your company
mentioned.

---

[28] Obscure is in the eyes of the beholder. I'm a movie buff and I'm
constantly quoting my favorite lines. It's great when people get it.
If we both recognize the line, it creates an immediate bond. But if I
quote Humphrey Bogart in Casablanca, "of all the gin joints in all
the towns in all the world she walks into mine," and the person I'm
talking to thinks I'm quoting a song by Fallout Boy, it only points
out our differences.

a. Use the site or publication's formal submission process, which is usually easy to find on the website. For example, for Techcrunch fill out the form at http://techcrunch.com/contact/, or

b. Email the blogger, author, or editor directly.

You can increase your chances of your story getting picked up by giving the blogger of your choice an exclusive on your story, along with credentials to use your prototype. Always give free access in exchange for coverage. When you do get press, tweet it out, post it to Facebook and update your LinkedIn status with it. Oh, also, get ready for thousands of hits on your site.

Mentor-driven Accelerators

The mentors you have reached out to probably have much larger networks than you do. It's fine to ask them to engage their networks to help get the word out. The level of promotion that this provides depends almost entirely on the mentor's reputation and the circles he or she runs in.

Mentor-driven accelerators (TechStars.org/network) are incredible ways to tap in to world-class mentors and investors *and* their networks of contacts. These programs are very competitive to get into, but if you are chosen, you are guaranteed a level of visibility and access that few could achieve on their own.

You give up some equity (e.g. 6% of common stock) in return for a small cash investment and a large investment of time and access to the kind of mentors and prospective investors that can help you progress to the next stage quickly. You have to decide if it's worth it, but the results speak for themselves. Most accelerator graduates get funded and go on to succeed. Of course you have to apply to get in and you are competing with a lot of other startups. But you have a big advantage – you've started fast, you've got a demo video and you already have a partially validated prototype. That will put you ahead of much of the competition to get into an accelerator.

> **Apply to a mentor-driven accelerator program**:
> - Go to TechStars.com/network and Techstars.com to review the available programs. You can also check out other accelerators like Y Combinator, Idealab, Dogpatchlabs and see which one best fits your needs and desires (e.g. location, schedule, deal).
> - Fill out the application on the accelerator site of your choice or at accelerato.rs
> - Pay attention to the fact that different accelerators have different foci and mentors. Pick the one(s) with the best fit to your business.
> - Make contact with the Managing Director(s) and look for opportunities to meet in person. Keep them informed by email of progress you make.

If you get selected by one of the accelerators, commit yourself fully to the process. Generally the program is three months, you move in to the accelerator's facility and work your tail off. You will get help and advice with every challenge but still make your own decisions. There is a very good chance that the experience will change your destiny dramatically for the better[29].

Business Plan Competitions

Another way to get exposure is to enter business plan competitions run by universities, venture capital groups and economic developers. These competitions provide visibility and an opportunity to win some cash. Don't write a "complete business plan." Just write down what you know (your value proposition, business model, results and customer feedback to date), what you've done so far and what you're going to do next.

---

[29] Full disclosure – my partner Nasir Ali and I are the Managing Directors of the StartFast Venture Accelerator (startfast.net) which is a member of the TechStars Network. Obviously I'm biased.

Workin' on my forecast!

Sometimes the judging in these competitions is a bit old-school MBA, but even if you don't win, you'll gain valuable exposure by going through the process. More and more, the people running and judging these competitions are in sync with the Lean Startup model and will appreciate the fact that you've got a prototype and some market feedback. Nonetheless, don't waste your valuable time guessing at a 5-year forecast or some other folly just to completely fill out the entry forms.

Validate

The purpose of putting out a minimum viable product (MVP) and promoting it is to get information about the fit between your current offering and the true needs of your market. Validation of market fit is crucial. At this point you need to separate *assumptions* about the needs of the target market from the *factual* needs of the market. The success or failure of your business rests on whether you achieve market fit quickly enough. Getting the MVP into the hands of users and demonstrating it to experts in the target market helps to validate what you've done right and ferret out what needs adjustment. Course correction at this stage is easier and less costly than when the product is more fully featured, larger and harder to debug.

As your early users work with your MVP, you need their help to refine the product's user experience - how the product fits into their everyday workflow. What is value to the customer of specific features? Early adopters tend to be rabid fans of new technology. They also appreciate having influence over the product's direction and getting what they ask for. Their love and loyalty are the most precious assets of the business at this stage (right up there with time and cash). Therefore treat your early users like royalty. Your business needs them more than they need you.

Regular face to face meetings with early local users will help you build productive relationships for getting fine points of user interface or product flow ironed out. Take user input but consider these two caveats:

1. Remember to test every new feature request against a market need. As much as you respect and need your early users' feedback, you're not building a custom product just for them.

2. Stick to your original vision stubbornly until it's clearly time to pivot. It often takes some time to prove-in your original concept and you don't want to get whip-sawed by users or mentors. Make adjustments, but don't deviate too far until it's clear that you must.

Aside from feedback from early users and mentors, how else can you gather information to tell you if you've designed a solution that people want, need and are willing to pay for? Two other useful techniques are analytics and user forums.

Analytics

Analytics will tell you how many people are visiting your site, where they are visiting from, how many conversions you're getting, and other useful statistics. I recommend implementing Google Analytics along with a tool like Chartbeat.com or ActiveConversion.com. These tools allow you to create custom landing pages targeted per community so that you can accurately monitor the effectiveness of each campaign.

You should also instrument your code to expose how many times the application is run, which features are being used most (and least), and how stable the application is. This approach will collect valuable data from all your users, not just the vocal minority.

User Forums

While analytics will give you an idea of the traffic you're generating, you definitely have a need for more qualitative feedback on your prototype and its features. At the same time, if you're getting hundreds or even thousands of users, you can't engage them all personally. User forums are a way to get users talking online to you and to each other. Your goal is to create and nurture not just a collection of users but rather a user *community*. For the practical details on creating an online forum go to phpbb.com or forumforfree.com.

In most user communities new users ask questions in the forum and the more experienced users answer them. You need to keep users engaged and also increase the number of users who are answering questions. Make sure that you are moderating the forum. Keep new users comfortable by implementing a no-tolerance policy on personal attacks or ridiculing questions.

You also want to encourage new users to start answering questions. There's no better way to learn something than to attempt to teach it. Write posts on how to answer other users' questions and resist the temptation to jump in and answer questions yourself. You'll get more involvement if users are talking to each other and not just to you.

Extend that zero-tolerance policy to ridiculing other people's answers too. Some technical forums are extremely harsh and have a culture where people get flamed regularly. You need to moderate that behavior out of your forum. You can't let a few egoists spoil the party, or you'll quickly get a user forum that is of little or no value.

If you can make a game out of asking and answering questions and reward people with badges or status in the forum, you'll engage more users. Let the person who asked the question rate the most useful answers. I also recommend rewards based on the volume of questions asked and answered with visible status. Encourage humor in the forum as long as it's not derogatory of another user or group.

Adjust to User Feedback

You initially gain traction through promotion, but you must listen and adapt quickly to your users' feedback or they'll drop you like a hot rock. Users may give you feedback on their experience dealing with your product or service (User Experience) and on your business model.

User Experience

Feedback on user experience might address *flow* or *features*. There are rules about what you should change and what you shouldn't.

Flow is the way a feature is implemented. How many clicks does it take to get a certain job done? Where are the controls located? What does the display look like? Is it attractive, easy to navigate and intuitive? Flow feedback is easy to respond to and you should implement flow improvements early and often. This is one way to delight your users. When you get suggestions on flow you should always take them, with one exception. If there are two users who give the opposite feedback from each other, you will obviously have to decide one way or the other.

Features are another matter entirely. Your MVP was released with only the absolutely necessary features. Your users will naturally ask for new features, and you should grant their requests, but be very careful while doing so. Adding too many features can detract from your product's usability. You're looking for an optimum. Add features that will satisfy your users, but not so many that your product gets cluttered or inefficient.

Every feature you add will need to be debugged, maintained and described in the manual and training for the product. Those activities cost money. If the new feature doesn't provide added value to your users, and differentiate you from your competitors, then it's a waste[30].

> *When you make something that works a little better, you're playing the same game, just keeping up with the status quo. When you make something different, on the other hand, you're trying to change the game.*
> *- Seth Godin, serial entrepreneur and author*

Before you add any feature, make it pass at least two of these three tests:

---

[30] I'm writing this book using Microsoft Word, a perfect example of software with too many features that don't add any value for me, the user. If I use 10% of them, I'd be surprised.

1. Will this new feature add value to your users? Will it save them time? Will it allow them to make more money? Make sure you understand how the feature will do these things for the user and implement it in a way that will surprise and delight them.

2. Is this feature required by your users to complete their desired task? Is it a must-have that somehow got left out of the MVP?

3. Relative to the competition, does this new feature allow the problem to be solved in a new and different way? Or is it just me-too? Don't get into playing catch-up ball. Find a way to think differently and change the game to your advantage.

Enhancing User Engagement

Why are video games, online games and social games addictive? What makes Facebook, Twitter, LinkedIn and Yelp so popular? These companies employ specific techniques to increase *user engagement* (the level at which users are motivated to spend their resources on the site or app). Start by collecting data on every user action so that you can determine what's working to motivate people to use your app or website. Use this analysis to adapt your product accordingly.

Humans evolved with an innate drive to solve survival problems. It is less clear how we came by our motivations to achieve higher-level objectives on Maslow's hierarchy, but they too seem to be deeply instinctive and psychological. Here is a list of ways that you can engage these drives to increase user engagement with your product or service:

1. Reduce the cost of participation. Make sign up easy (and free if your business model allows it).

2. Create a means to measure users' reputations. LinkedIn has recommendations; eBay has seller ratings; Amazon has reviews.

3. Reward users for their efforts (trying) in small increments with no punishment for failure. In World of Warcraft (WoW) and other games you get experience points for trying, even if you don't accomplish the goal. In Yelp you earn badges. These are all means of offering users recognition.

4. Wanting is more motivating than liking. People are more engaged when they are working toward a goal (wanting) than when they achieve a desired goal (liking). Provide an ongoing series of steps (15-20 steps is optimal) required for users to hit a target. If there are multiple long and short-term aims, giving the user a choice of which to work on at any given time, your site can hold their interest for a long time.

5. Give immediate, clear, frequent feedback. Progress bars or counters that update every time an action is taken are most effective.

6. <u>In games, random reinforcement is powerful</u>. Give a small reward (like finding a useful object in WoW) about 25% of the time so the user will not be frustrated or find it too easy. Once a user nears a goal (e.g. finishing a level), increase the probability of success to 75%. About 10% of the time the reward given should be better than average and 0.1% of the time, the reward should be truly awesome. After an awesome reward make sure it doesn't happen again for some time. Follow these guidelines and your game should be addictive.

7. <u>Create community</u>. People like to watch others doing things (e.g. Facebook). We like to have others watching us (e.g. YouTube). People like to do things together collaboratively (e.g. WoW). To increase engagement, create elements that measure reputation (e.g. ratings, comments, "likes"), popularity (e.g. followers, fans), and other rankings. Create a social pressure or cost for not participating regularly (e.g. email from Facebook: "Chuck, you have notifications pending.)"

Business Model Adjustments

Adjustments to your business model may also be requested by customers. For example, listen very carefully to the feedback, "You need some additional tiers of service between your Free version and the currently cheapest paid version." This is very common feedback, but you need to model the likely outcome. What are your costs to acquire, maintain, and support a customer? Would the proposed new tiers of service be profitable? How many additional free customers could you convert to paying if you had those additional tiers? These questions can be answered by testing them out in a portion of your market on the next iteration.

You will likely be asked to lower your pricing. Again this is a complex question. Is your demand elastic with price (will you get more paying customers if you lower your pricing), or inelastic (should you raise your prices because you'll have the same number of customers either way)? It's difficult to know if you haven't tested either hypothesis. If you're funded, you'll probably be focused on the maximum velocity of customer acquisition, so you won't raise your prices. But if you're still largely self-funded, you need to look at profitability and cash flow too. Model your options in a spreadsheet and engage mentors to give you feedback in making this type of decision.

In general, you should be responsive to requests to tweak your business model. For example, LegalZoom added free live consultation with lawyers on staff to their value proposition in response to overwhelming customer feedback asking for it. It turns out that they sell more if the customers are comfortable that they can get help when they ask for it. If it's affordable and helps your customers, then do it.

Iterate[31]

The process I've just described never really ends. It changes its character as the product and market mature, but in general, it's a good idea to always put your customers first, respond to their needs and continually make your product or service better and better. However there is a point where you can say that your product/market fit is good enough to begin scaling the business. You know that you have product/market fit when the customers start coming to you and your growth rate is accelerating without any additional effort or promotion. When this happens, you can begin to make reasonable forecasts of your business. When you can forecast the two quarters ahead and come within 10-20% above or below your forecast, you're ready for the next step - financing and scaling the business.

---

[31] I've always loved recursion.

CHAPTER 5 – FINANCING & SCALING

"The investor of today does not profit from yesterday's growth."
- Warren Buffet, Berkshire Hathaway Chairman & CEO

"You can get the code right, you can get the products right, but you need to get the culture right first. If you don't get the culture right then your company won't scale."
- Aditya Agarwal, Facebook Director of Engineering

By now, investors are probably approaching you. And that's a good thing because you're strapped for cash. Growth consumes cash. If your business is successful, you'll need money to finance the very process of growing. Guess what? You're under-capitalized. How do you get the money, people, processes and infrastructure you need to scale? Let's start with money.

How to meet prospective investors

> *"The best time to plant a tree is twenty years ago, the second best time is now."*
> *- Anonymous*

The best time to raise money is before you need it. Likewise the best time to meet prospective investors is before you need them. If you've implemented my advice so far by going to Startup Weekends, Meetup groups, entrepreneur roundtables and business plan competitions, then you already know a few investors. Investor groups hold events every month. If you enrolled in a startup accelerator, then you have been exposed to a lot of investors. If you haven't done these things, then it's time to do them now. It's much easier to approach an investor you already know. Otherwise, you will need to be introduced to that investor by someone you both know.

Before meeting with prospective investors do your homework. Read *Venture Deals* by Brad Feld and Jason Mendelson. Study the investor's website as well as CrunchBase.com. Make sure they have money and are currently making investments in companies like yours (same industy, market and stage) in amounts close to what you need to raise.

Market Positioning

How do explain to a prospective investor where you and your product or service sits relative to the rest of the market? A *Market Landscape Chart* shows on one page the companies in your market, their positions and relationships. Prepare one before meeting investors.

Start by naming your market (e.g. Cloud Infrastructure). Divide the chart vertically into "swim lanes," one for each major segment of the market. In the example I've listed Colocation and Web Hosting, Storage, Platform and Apps. Another market would break down a different way. Experiment until you get a breakdown that makes sense to you.

Market Landscape Chart (step 1)

Next place your company and others of which you are aware into position in the landscape. Add your partners, your competitors, your competitors' partners. Just try to get them into the right swim lane; it doesn't matter yet where they are in the lane. If you find a company that doesn't fit into any of your swim lanes you may need to add a new lane or rename a lane to be more general. There may be some companies that fit into more than one swim lane. For example, Google provides storage, platform and apps (e.g. Google Docs). Likewise Apple, Microsoft Azure and Amazon Web Services are more than just platforms. You can show this visually by stretching these companies to overlap multiple swim lanes. Now your chart will look something like this:

Market Landscape Chart (step 2)

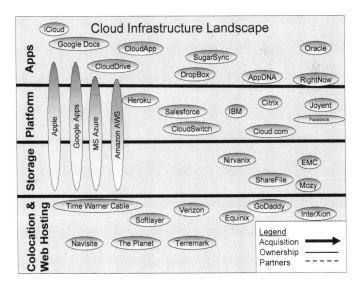

Now it's time to make refinements to the chart to show relationships, mergers and acquisitions, and to add any missing companies that you need to illustrate your point.

CloudApp is built upon AWS, with a platform called Heroku. You can show this relationship by coloring all three the same shade or using a dotted line to connect platforms or partners. Heroku is also related to the Salesforce platform so there is a dotted line there.

Next you can add in major acquisitions. This is an important part of the landscape chart because it shows which companies are acting to consolidate the space. In this case, we see Verizon acquiring Terremark and CloudSwitch, clearly trying to build a multi-tier platform to compete with the other vertically integrated clouds. Citrix is doing the same thing at a higher level by acquiring Cloud.com, ShareFile and AppDNA. Several other acquisitions are shown as well, all in one chart.

When the landscape chart is complete you can see at a glance who the players are, their relationships and who is placing bets through acquisitions. You can also record your company's position and partnerships in this context. This chart gives you valuable insight into the market and shows your investors that you know where you fit as well as who your potential acquirers might be. Be creative, but remember that you'll be using this chart to communicate with other people, so make sure you don't deviate too far from the common consensus in your definitions.

Market Landscape Chart (step 3)

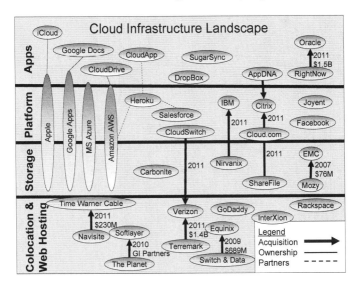

As you hear of new companies in your space, just add them to the chart. Landscape charts are living documents. They can get very crowded and you'll probably use a full page with smaller bubbles and fonts for the companies. It's OK to put down only the companies that are relevant to you. It will make the picture much clearer without extraneous information.

Some of the companies in the landscape are your competitors. These need to be singled out for special attention.

Competitive Analysis

A competitive analysis is not only needed to explain to your investors how you intend to win business, it will help you identify what you have to focus on to compete effectively. I recommend being very specific and doing a competitive analysis for each market segment in which you participate. Different market segments may have different competitors and buying criteria.

The choice of criteria is yours, but make sure you include everything your customers have told you is important to them. Why did they choose your product or service over the competition? What factors entered into the decisions of the customers you didn't win or those that switched from your product or service to a competitor's?

Make a competitive analysis spreadsheet: In the rows, list your company followed by the competitors that customers in your target market segment have the choice to buy from. Across the top, list the features or other factors that might influence a customer's decision to buy from you or someone else. These could be features, functions, benefits, or any other differentiator you or one of your competitors has. Price is always a factor. If you know what % share of the market you or your competition has, write it down as well. Fill in the boxes as best you can, either with a check or blank or with a number or description.

Once you've defined your competitive criteria and filled in the cells your competitive analysis spreadsheet will look something like this:

Competitive Analysis Spreadsheet

	SaaS	Easy	GUI	Support	Price	Market Share
YoYoTech	✓	✓	✓		$1	0.1%
Competitor A	✓			✓	$10	20%
Competitor B		✓		✓	$5	20%
Competitor C		✓	✓	✓	$0.50	60%

For example, suppose your company, YoYoTech, has competitors A, B and C for your Software as a Service (SaaS) offering. Yoyotech's differentiators are ease of use and a nice looking graphic user interface (GUI). YoYoTech's customers don't need much support since the product is so intuitive, which allows you to charge a lower price ($1 per user per month) than most of your competitors. You've just started, so your market share is small (0.1%) so far.

Competitor A also offers a SaaS solution, but theirs is complex, hard to use and has a text-based user interface. They make up for this by providing excellent technical support and charge a lot more ($10 per user per month). They've built a significant market share (20%) by taking business away from their competition (B&C) who sell software licenses which need to installed on the user's computer.

Competitor B's software is easy to use, but lacks a graphic user interface. They have lost the most market share to Competitor A - customers that prefer a SaaS model to a license model. To compare prices we need to divide the license fee that B charges by the estimate of the number of users and number of months the license is useful for. In this case, we estimate B's price to be the equivalent of $5 per user per month.

Competitor C is the market leader, with 60% market share. Their software is easy to use, has a nice GUI and they provide excellent customer support. They sell to large corporations so even though their licenses cost a lot, their effective cost per user per month is only $0.50.

By looking at this spreadsheet you can easily see where you need to focus to beat your competition as well as how they intend to beat you. For example, you could target smaller businesses that Competitor C isn't interested in. Your lower cost per user relative to A and B, combined with your SaaS model, ease of use and GUI should help you compete effectively and win market share over time.

This too is a living document. Add new competitors as they come into the market and adjust the necessary factors as your competition makes changes to their offering. Add new criteria as you learn more about your customer's preferences. And make a new competitive analysis for each new Target Market you pursue as you grow.

Finally, make sure your company is financeable before you approach prospective investors.

Not every company is financeable

"Intellectuals solve problems, geniuses prevent them."
- Albert Einstein

The absolute minimum requirements for your business to attract any kind of investment are (in order of importance):

1. <u>A strong team</u>. Are all the key ingredients there? Do you have passion, integrity and the ability to execute?

2. <u>The market</u>. Is the opportunity large? Is there a way to break in? Do we have something unique (differentiated)?

3. <u>The business model</u>. Is there an attractive way to make money (eventually)?

If any of these three things is broken, then it's going to be hard to raise capital. But even when these three basic stars are aligned, there are lots of other potential deal-killers. Here are some common ones.

The company doesn't own its intellectual property

It's normal and customary for founders to assign their intellectual property rights to the company in exchange for their shares. It's a bad sign if an investor has to tell you that when you're trying to raise financing. Have that conversation early and get the signatures of each founder. Make sure that any contractor that works on the product also signs a "work for hire" agreement that assigns all rights and ownership to the company. Investors want assurance that the company's intellectual property is solely and exclusively owned by the company and is locked down as much as possible. If there is any question, argument or ambiguity on this point, your company will be unfinanceable until it is fixed.

Avoid (fix) IP issues:
- Have all founders assign their invention rights to the company in writing in exchange for their shares.
- Have any contractors involved in development assign their rights in writing to the company.
- Make a list of third-party rights (e.g. licensed software, open-source software) that might impact your company's ownership of its product.
- Have a mentor (an intellectual property attorney if possible) review your IP situation and tell you if you're ready to approach investors.

I've seen some crazy terms in outsourced development contracts where the contractor claimed ownership of the code they would write for the client. Don't sign an agreement like this. The contractor may need to be able to reuse elements of the solution they write for you, but you must have ownership of the work product you contract for. Who would invest in your company if you don't own the product or service?

The company doesn't own its market

"First of all, no one in their right mind would sign an exclusive contract."
- Rob Walton

The word "exclusivity" is almost always a problem. It mystifies me how often companies I'm advising want to sign some kind of exclusive agreement with a partner. If you do, consider that you're pretty much selling the company at that point, because nobody else will buy it (or invest in it) while that exclusive contract is in place. Now before you start arguing with me, let me just say that I know your situation is unique. That's why you have mentors. Please seek their council before signing anything exclusive.

The point is that any kind of contract that is one-sided or "commercially unfavorable" to your company can potentially make your business unfinanceable. Every contract should have a way out. Never sign a contract that gives someone else unilateral (one-sided) control over your destiny. Your right to choose markets, set pricing and generate profits from your technology, products and services should never be signed away to someone else.

> Never sign any license, partnership, agreement or contract of an exclusive nature, especially if it is difficult or expensive to terminate.

As obvious as this may seem, it is all too common – so much so that there are numerous clichés for this kind of thing:

- Selling yourself short
- Mortgaging your company's future
- Giving away the store
- Betting the farm

The owners don't work here anymore

One technology company I advised had been around a while and had paid a lot of people with stock. Their cap table (the list of shareholders and their equity holdings in the company) was a long list of former employees, former co-founders, contractors, partners, etc. This kind of situation complicates things for investors and can be a red flag.

Co-founders should agree on who owns what shares and what happens if one of the founders leaves. This can be simple, (e.g. "we each own a third, but if one of us has to bail before we get funded, that one forfeits his or her shares") or complex, but it has to be specific and in writing. Unless you've done this kind of thing before, this is a very good place to get a mentor's advice.

You really want to avoid having someone you *used to* work with owning a big chunk of the company. You should also avoid making any promises to pay others with equity until you're large enough to set up an employee option plan. Ambiguity and complexity regarding the legal ownership of the company is the enemy. Clarity and simplicity are your friends.

Your entrance is my exit

During the early days of your venture, you will undoubtedly spend some money. If you start fast and follow the guidelines in this book, you'll spend a lot less than you would otherwise, but you're still going to be out of pocket some cash. Sometimes founders, often on the advice of their attorneys or accountants, record their expenses as shareholder loans to the company. Sometimes founders put the salary they'd like to be making, if only the company were far enough along to pay it, on the books as "deferred compensation."

Let me be absolutely clear. You are not going to get paid back by your investors for shareholder loans and deferred compensation. Investors want their capital to go to moving the company forward, not to repaying the founders. If you're in this situation, convert your loans into equity[32] before you start raising capital. Otherwise, you're wasting time, putting an unnecessary obstacle in place, and making yourself look naïve (at best) to prospective investors.

Obviously it's best to avoid these kinds of problems by paying attention to them up front. Use your common sense, advice from mentors and professional help when needed to solve the rest after the fact.

Debt or Equity

Investors provide cash in the hope of receiving more money in return at a future time. When you accept their cash you enter into a *debt* or *equity* arrangement that defines the terms of the relationship until the investor has gotten their return on investment. Debt is simply a loan that you must pay back at a future time. Convertible debt is a loan that can be paid back by converting it into some number of shares at a future time. Equity means the investor buys stock and becomes a part-owner just like you.

---

[32] Ask a mentor who is an attorney or accountant to help you with this. It is fairly straightforward, but there are enough variables and consequences that if you don't have an appropriately skilled mentor, it's worth getting some professional advice.

How much is the company worth?

Equity financing for early stage companies forces a valuation (a calculation of what the company is worth) before it is really possible to determine. There are excellent methods of valuing companies that generate profits and positive cash flow. There's a formula called the Discounted Cash Flows method or DCF that is pretty well accepted in most cases. Unfortunately, you're probably not able to provide the necessary inputs for this formula[33]. You'll need to fall back on some other method:

- Negotiation: The company is worth exactly what a buyer (the investor) and a seller (you) agree it's worth after negotiation.

- Comparables: The company is worth some range of values that similar companies at a similar stage have sold for to similar investors on similar terms recently.

- Rules of thumb: Examples: 5-8 times EBITDA[34] or 2-3 times annual revenues (either trailing twelve months or projected).

- Expected Return: The investor's expectation of return can be expressed as a spreadsheet

---

[33] Like a five-year cash flow forecast that's more than a guess.

[34] Earning Before Tax Depreciation and Amortization – a measure of profitability. Pronounced 'ē-bǐt-dä'.

formula. Calculate the Net Present Value (discounted for risk) of the future exit valuation of the company. The result varies widely depending upon how much risk is assessed and your guess of when and what the exit valuation will be.

Many entrepreneurs value their startup at 10 times the amount of money they need to raise because they are emotionally comfortable with giving up 10% equity. There is no reason for an investor to respect that kind of thinking. It's about as useful as the investor valuing the company so that whatever amount they invest, they get 51% ownership. Try out the various methods of valuation to get a range of values that have some justification. In the end, the investor's connections and their ability to engage them may be more important to your business than the deal.

He said we're worth "Big Bucks"!

If it's too early to decide on a valuation, one way to avoid (well delay, actually) the whole imbroglio is to use convertible debt. This is a loan that converts to stock when some future event happens (like the company raises capital by selling equity and therefore there is a valuation). Usually the early investor wants a discount at that future time to whatever later investors pay.

For example, YoYoTech needs $100,000 to launch their next gen product and I lend it to them under a convertible note, converting to equity with a 30% discount over the next round. A year later, YoYoTech gets a venture capital firm (VC) to invest $1,000,000 for 10% of the company, meaning that the premoney valuation is $10,000,000. So my $100,000 converts to 1.3% of YoYoTech plus any interest I've earned. Convertible notes are a great tool for both entrepreneurs and investors to start fast because the longer you wait to put a value on your company, the better the chance that you'll have enough relevant information to do so rationally.

The choice of debt, equity or convertible debt is usually up to the investor. Be open to and prepared for all possibilities.

How to make your company worth more

There are several things you can do to make your business more attractive and valuable in the eyes of investors. It's best to apply this list ahead of any investment pitch.

1. Have a product or service that people are using and is generating some revenue.

2. If possible relate how your product or service will help your customers make more money, save money, change their lives for the better or even save their lives.

3. Identify the larger market even if you're currently targeting a niche. Fast growing markets are best.

4. Know who your competitors are and how you're different.

5. Have a written sales and marketing plan outlining proven, cost-effective go-to-market tactics and a clear idea of who your customers are.

6. Have a forecast of how your business will grow over the next 2-3 years.

7. Get intellectual property agreements in place with the team. File patents on key technologies (you'll need mentor help here).

8. Make sure your team has entrepreneurial and domain expertise and that you have invested a lot of your own time and money into the company. Be prepared to hire a senior financial person (or a fractional CFO) to look after the millions you're about to raise.

9. Use a well-respected corporate attorney, intellectual property attorney and accounting firm. Make sure you can pay them from the proceeds of the financing.

10. Know the kinds of deals that your VC does, the companies they've invested in and the valuations of those companies. Be prepared to

draw parallels between those deals and your situation.

11. Don't propose a crazy valuation, even as a starting point. There's a very good chance you're not the next Facebook. Let the investor start that part of the conversation.

Angels and Demons

There are stages of investing just like there are stages of development of your startup. Roughly these stages are known as Pre-seed, Seed, A-round, B-round, and Later Stage.

The Pre-seed stage is what this book has been about thus far. You are funding the company yourself, maybe with some help from friends and family. Perhaps you can raise some cash from a business plan competition, or revenues from early customers. Once you take investment capital (whether debt or equity) from strangers, you've moved to the Seed stage.

Seed stage investors are often individuals or groups of individuals called "angels." There are only a few very early stage venture capital firms. The seed round is typically less than $1 million, and may be as low as $10,000 - $50,000. Seed stage investors are primarily looking for a great team and a good market. In today's market there may actually be several rounds of seed financing, follow-on rounds and bridge loans before a professional venture capital fund invests.

The first institutional round of capital into the company is called Series A. The amount raised in a series A varies widely but is typically in the $2-10 million range. Both the company and the Series A investors intend that it's enough money to finance the company to become successful, profitable and cash flow positive. At this point the company can survive indefinitely. The investors are betting that a profitable exit can be found which gives them a big return on their capital.

Before raising a Series A, you should have figured out your product and have some traction in the market. Optimally, the purpose of the Series A money should be to scale and adapt the business model in order to develop product / market fit. For example, how and with whom do you go to market (direct or through distribution) and how do you optimize customer acquisition? How do you expand into new geographies and vertical markets? You should also use the A round to refine and optimize your business model – that is to figure out how to make money at scale.

Series B is the next step in the funding cycle, averaging $7 million and up[35]. Sometimes the purpose is to fund acquisitions, sometimes for expansion. If the core team

---

[35] In October 2011, DropBox raised a $250 million B round (maybe the largest to date), presumably to fund acquisitions.

has executed well and the product is successfully and rapidly gaining market share, then Series B is about scaling the business as fast as possible. Perhaps you need to hire sales and marketing or customer service people. Maybe your business is doing great in the US and Europe and you need to expand into Asia. Maybe you need to scale inorganically (e.g. by buying a partner or competitor). By this stage you have market traction (users are finding you) and you also have a business model that has come together to produce significant cash flow.

If the company is not doing well, then Series B can be about replacing the founders[36] and funding a new

---

[36] In my second startup we created software called SmartMaps (which converted scanned maps into an object oriented database) and later FastGate (mobile app for intelligent field data collection). Seed funding came from Niagara Mohawk Power Corp (NMPC now National Grid). After several iterations from prototype to product with early adopters at NMPC, we launched on a national scale. Based on market feedback, we pivoted and became a service provider, operating our software for power companies around the country. Within a year we raised a $2 million Series A round from St. Paul Venture Capital (now Vesbridge).

We recruited and relocated a VP Sales, who had a massive heart attack early in his tenure and was out for 6 months. We held his job for him while my co-founders and I tried to pick up the slack. I refused to lay off employees when business inevitably slowed and we burned cash as a result. In short order, we needed a bridge round of another $1 million and then brought in JAFCO America fund for a $3 million Series B.

management team to fix what's broken. Investors with millions of dollars at stake want experienced executives at the helm, especially if the founding team is topping out (reaching the limits of their ability to execute). Most investors maintain a pool of executive talent available to take over if and when the founding execs stumble in

---

The plan with the new money was to acquire other map conversion companies to scale quickly. We acquired a French company, Network Management Group (NMG), which began hemorrhaging cash and we needed more capital to fund its losses. Series C was a "down round" and I was asked to step down from CEO to President in favor of an older executive recruited by the VC's.

With every new CEO comes a new round of capital. I raised a Series D round of $9.9 million from The Beacon Group, a VC fund formed by former Goldman Sachs execs. The VC's now had controlling interest in the company. The new CEO built and staffed an expensive executive office we didn't need near his home in Chicago (the company was in Syracuse), brought in new sales and marketing execs that knew nothing about the utility industry, and didn't stem the increasing tide of negative cash flow from France. Within 18 months the cash was gone, he was fired, and the company's sales had shrunk by 40%.

The VC's brought in another new CEO, an astute businessman with whom I became good friends. In fact, I chose to work with him again for many years thereafter. The investors put another $5 million in (the E round) to support the new CEO and with it we were able to stabilize and find a buyer for the US business. On the strength of our technology and the brilliance of my co-founders and the technical team, we were able to get $20 million cash from a private utility services company. The company I founded and built went on without me, and still exists to this day. I chose to go with the new CEO to clean up the mess in France. But that's another story.

execution. This is quite often the case, since the game has changed and now many of the things that made the company successful in the first place – disruption, innovation, experimentation – may no longer be required. The mission after a Series B is all about scale - the faster the climb the better.

Choosing Investors

At the early stages of your business, you have the power to make good decisions about who you're going to work with and that includes investors. One of the best reasons for using as little capital as possible in the beginning is that you'll be able to take the time to choose wisely rather than taking any willing investor that comes along out of desperation or necessity.

The biggest difference between choosing seed (very early) stage venture investors, A-round investors and later stage investors is that it will be easier to get information about established funds through research. Definitely spend time finding out everything you can online and then fill in the gaps by asking the investor questions. Here's what you need and want to know before engaging in due diligence[37] with any stage of venture investor.

---

[37] Due diligence is the process the investor uses to find out everything there is to know about you and your company prior to investing. It's usually the most time-consuming part, and so

Where is the fund in their lifecycle? Venture funds also raise money. The fund is the General Partner and they have Limited Partners (LPs) who put up the cash. The best time to raise money from a venture firm is when its funds are fresh. Find out from which Fund the firm will invest in you, the size of the fund, when the money was raised and when the LPs expect their returns. Some funds are "evergreen," investing an annual flow of money from some other enterprise, but they too will have policies effecting the time horizon of their investments. Find out what those are. Individual angels may be investing from their own funds and have longer time horizons, but you should still get a clear understanding of their expectations.

How well does your company fit the investor's thesis? Are you at the right stage, in the right vertical market, using the set of technologies they prefer and understand? One way to answer these questions is to look at the portfolio of companies in which they've already invested and see if you are similar to them when the investments were made. These answers will be indicative of both how likely you are to get money from this investor and how much value the investor can add.

---

shouldn't be engaged in until you're comfortable with that investor.

Find out who will sit on your board of directors, how many other boards they are on, their background, track record and other details. Will they have enough time to be a valuable addition to the board or just enough to observe and report? Do they have contacts in your industry that can help you move the business forward? What have they done before that will complement the rest of the board?

Meet the investors in person before going too far into the process. Do you feel comfortable in their presence or not? It's natural to be a little nervous when meeting someone new, but beyond that, what's your gut reaction? If there were no money involved, would you recruit this person as a mentor? If not, then do you really want them sitting on your board and overseeing every major decision from now on? Do you want to share ownership with them in one of the most important parts of your life?

Speak with founders of other companies in which this investor has invested. What were their experiences? What is the investor like when there are disagreements, high-pressure situations, and reversals of fortune? Find out everything you can about the investor's character. There will undoubtedly be difficult times in your relationship and behavior under stress is often very different than during the courting process. It would also be prudent to speak with a founder whose position in the business changed after investment. This happens frequently, most often for good reason and to the benefit of all parties concerned. Nonetheless it will help to get another founder's unemotional perspective on how they were treated by the investors.

Just like marriages entered into blindly or hastily, unwise investor / founder relationships often end badly. If you are not happy with what you find out as you explore the answers to the above questions, I advise you have an open conversation with the prospective investor about it. You may learn more about them and yourself in that conversation which will help you make a good decision. It may be best to keep looking until you find a source of funds that is a better fit[38]. Keep in mind, it is better to start building relationships with prospective investors long before you need their money.

---

[38] When my first startup Coherent Research, Inc. was looking for seed funding to get our Content Addressable Memory into production, there were very few local investors who understood the business. I met with several bright lights in the Silicon Valley venture capital community and it was clear that they would invest, but only if we moved the company to California. We turned them down and carefully selected a pair of local angel investors to invest alongside friends and family. These angels were incredibly supportive and added more value to the business, investing not just money, but large amounts of their personal time.

Swing at the first pitch

Now here is something that seems deeply paradoxical at first. Once you've decided that an investor has the right fit with you qualitatively (character, investment thesis, value add, time horizon) it might be a good idea to take the first deal you get offered. I call this swinging at the first pitch, because as in baseball, the first offer is sometimes the best one you're going to see all game. Of course that doesn't mean you should accept a crazy-low valuation or ridiculous terms. It just means to take the first offer seriously and avoid the common mistake of raising your deal expectations with the confidence that comes from having an offer in hand. Take the first reasonable deal you are offered by a reputable investor. Doing so will save you time (precious to a startup) and it will start the relationship with the investor out right (you're reasonable and easy to work with). That's worth much more than some optimization of valuation or terms at this stage of the game.

Riding the Whirlwind

> *"Anything you build on a large scale or with intense passion invites chaos."*
> *- Francis Ford Coppola, producer, director, screenwriter*

Once your product or service begins to be adopted by mainstream customers, your company will go into a hypergrowth phase, often called being "inside the tornado" after the Geoffrey Moore book by the same name[39]. The challenges at this stage are very different from the early startup days and they may hit the company so quickly that there is barely time to react. There is certainly no time for thoughtful reflection. So what do you need to do in advance to prepare yourself and your company for the rigors of success?

Leadership in each stage of growth of your company requires different talents and skills. The strengths that got you through the early startup days may actually be weaknesses during later stages. Every successful founder faces this challenge. Your ability to adapt will be tested. If you don't want to or can't adapt fast enough, then it is right and proper that you move aside and let others lead. New leaders may not be more adaptable than you - they may simply be better suited to the challenges your company is having *now*. If this happens, you can find a different role in the company which is more appropriate for you. On the other hand,

---

[39] *Crossing the Chasm* and *Inside the Tornado*, written by Geoffrey Moore twenty years ago are required reading for entrepreneurs. They give excellent advice on how a company's marketing tactics must change as it moves from stage to stage. But they are must-reads because their metaphors are deeply embedded into the speech and culture of venture capital in this country. If you haven't read these books, you can't really understand what VCs and serial entrepreneurs are talking about.

if you're up for extreme adaptation, you can keep your leadership position and grow with the job[40].

So what's it like? How do you grow with the job? When should you willingly step aside or help recruit your boss? Let's take this stage by stage.

When you first start the company, you and your co-founders necessarily have to do everything yourselves. The traits that make you excellent in that context are creativity, efficiency, industriousness and lack of sleep. Problems are best solved by the one who noticed them without an excess of discussion. Roles are fluid and permeable. There is so much to do and you have be prepared to do anything. At this stage, execution is about making things happen.

Once you've got your prototype launched and the company begins to grow, you face your first adaptation challenge. Doing what needs to be done is no longer enough because that approach by itself doesn't scale.

---

[40] I've had a lot of experience with this process. In my first venture I was the technical co-founder and grew into CEO. The second venture I co-founded, I started out as CEO, working with a brilliant technical co-founder. In the third company I co founded, my role evolved from CTO to head of Business Development to Sales and Marketing as the needs of the business evolved. In the startup I'm doing right now, I'm the business guy (Salesperson), working with a couple of co-founders who are the technical and domain expert respectively.

There quickly becomes more work than it is possible for you and your co-founders to do, so you bring in other people to help. Unlike you and your co-founders, these people need to be managed, and this adds a layer of complexity to your business. Are you a good manager? How quickly can you become one?

A good manager sets direction, delegates authority, and makes sound decisions in the presence of incomplete data. The key difference is that for the most part, teams of people are doing the detailed work, not individuals. Coordinating teams requires planning, documentation, review and communication. Delegating successfully requires the flexibility to let people do things their own way, as long as they get results[41].

---

[41] I had a tough time with this transition the first time two times I went through it. I wanted everyone we hired to be just like me and expected them to be as driven and committed as I was. I was used to working every night and weekend and I couldn't understand why everyone we hired didn't have the same work-ethic. I was not a good manager, even though I strived to be and for the most part thought I was. When projects got behind or when the results weren't to my liking, I tended to take over or micromanage. When this didn't work, I would swing to the opposite pole and be too hands-off (delegating isn't the same as "abdicating"). I did learn and adapt, but it was painful for both me and the people working with me. It took years before I could really appreciate the fine balance that is required and the true meaning of Peter Drucker's saying, *"Good management is a gift to those who receive it."*

Once you enter the hypergrowth phase, where your company is on the way to becoming a market leader, there are a whole new set of challenges. In this phase (which usually follows a series A financing) your company has to hire people to run customer support, sales and marketing, project management, professional services and other functions. You will be expanding the management team and probably recruiting a CFO. You will have outside investors on the Board. If you are running the company, you now have to be adept at recruiting, team building, communicating the vision to new employees, communicating results and challenges to the Board, forecasting, planning and making financial decisions. You need a management system that your staff can implement that gives you the dashboard required to set and adjust your course. Your management style needs to evolve as you become more of a coach now that you have managers reporting to you.

It's wonderful if you've been through this experience before and know what to expect from yourself and others. If not, then you'll just have to do your best. Business books can help[42], but you might not have time to read them. Mentors are very helpful here, but as the

---

[42] *Leading at the Speed of Growth: Journey from Entrepreneur to CEO*, by Katherine Catlin and Jana Matthews is an excellent source for a deeper understanding of this process.

challenges have evolved, you might also need some new mentors that can help with what you're going through now.

The best advice I can give you is to trust your instincts. If your heart and gut tell you one thing and your mind is confused or uncertain, go with your heart and gut. Never compromise on questions of integrity. Emotions are a different matter. If you have a strong emotional reaction to anything that's going on, do not act on it while you're having the emotion. Walk it off, get some perspective, talk to your trusted advisors and then take the appropriate action.

So when should you step aside and let someone else lead? That's a tough question. If you and your trusted advisors agree that you should, then it might be time to pass the reins. If you're miserable doing what you're doing and want to go back to a role to which you were better suited, it's probably time to do just that. If you find your emotions getting the better of you in business situations, then maybe you need a change. There are no pat answers for this one. Don't be misled into thinking that you need to run the company to have a good outcome. Likewise don't believe that if you pass leadership on to someone else you have to either leave the company or become subservient. There is a fine balance in being part of a team just as there is in leading one.

Scaling Your Technology

When you scale your business you are going to get lots of users. Every bug in your code now costs you a thousand times as much in support calls. Anything you used to do manually is suddenly untenable. The creative spark that led you to design a brilliant new software product will not necessarily help make that product viable at scale.

In order to scale your technology, you'll need someone on the team who has done it before. Look for talent with experience in scaling architecture, load balancing web servers, media servers and web services, clustered file systems, caching and database systems. The specific technologies will depend upon your application, but there are some common threads to consider.

Iterate your technology

It's not just your business model that needs iteration. Each time the number of users of your system increases by an order of magnitude (10, 100, 1000, 10,000, 100,000, 1,000,000, 10,000,000, 100,000,000) your solution will need to be rearchitected at some level. For example, if you are building a web site, you'll probably start with PHP[43] because it is simple to use

---

[43] PHP is a free server-side scripting language which is embedded into HTML and interpreted by a web server to generate a dynamic web page. PHP stands for "PHP Hypertext Preprocessor."

and quite flexible. However by the time you need
hundreds of web servers, you may find that PHP will
run out of gas. That doesn't mean you shouldn't start
with PHP. It means you need to be prepared to throw
out obsolete code when scale demands it.

At the beginning, time to market drives you to employ
the quickest solution to implement the feature you
need. For example, you might decide to store photos or
other images as objects in MySQL or another database
to make them easier to manipulate in your system. But
as you get hundreds, thousands and then millions of
them the database will break down[44].

There are some optimizations you can do without
throwing out your architecture entirely and starting
over. For example, if you're delivering video, audio, or
other large files, a Content Delivery Network (CDN)
can be bolted on to your solution fairly easily. CDNs
are service providers that you pay to cache your content
in their media servers around the world and then
deliver them on demand to users. As such they charge
you for the bandwidth used, so your profitability will be
affected. But this is usually more than offset by the

---

[44] This happened recently when we used a partner's web content
management solution, designed for the education market, for
professionals in content creation. The size and sheer number of
media files brought the database to its knees. To scale, we had to
abandon that architecture and build a new solution.

speed with which a CDN can help you scale and the fact that you don't have to buy the capital equipment and build the solution yourself.

Don't take a bazooka to game of darts

Focus on your product or service and only make the changes that are required to scale. The key is to figure out what needs optimization and what needs to be completely re-architected. Remember it is an iterative process, so it's OK to build short term fixes and then replace them later.

In some cases you may need to replace PHP, Jquery or other interpreted code with optimized C++ that you write yourself and compile. You may be able to store objects more compactly (which will give your application savings in both time and memory) in C++ than in Python or Ruby.

On the other hand, there are so many different open source solutions available, you can almost always find a starting point that someone else has worked out. For example, maybe replacing Apache with NGINX will solve the immediate scaling issues you're having. Make sure you've exhausted the available problem solving options before you go inventing your own compiler or database. Remember that when you invent your own components or services you will have to cover deployment, monitoring, operations and interfaces and that takes time.

Scaling occurs across multiple dimensions and you can't always predict which type of growth is going to occur. Thus to some extent you have to react quickly to facts and patterns of use rather than trying to implement the ultimate scalable architecture up front. Otherwise you'll spend time and money on resources that may not ever be used. You'll need to pay attention to what the bulk of your users are doing so that you can choose which scaling battles to fight now and which to leave for another day.

Start Fast and Do More Faster

In scaling as with other things remember that the nature of a lean startup is to experiment, measure the outcome and try again. Set a focused team on a scaling challenge and let them run. It's OK to break things and fix them as needed. If you let people innovate you'll attract and retain the best people. Since scaling is a constant iterative process, your best and smartest developers should always be thinking about what they have to do next. They will never run out of creative challenges and that's what keeps the great ones motivated.

In the old days, we'd test a release candidate for months before releasing it. Now that seems like a dinosaur's approach. What can you break in the lab? You can simulate load, but you can't accurately simulate or predict what the actual internet and millions of individual users are going to do to your solution. As you modify your code base, definitely do unit testing before putting new code into production. But this can be done daily or weekly. If you're making a larger change, having a group of beta users test the new code before releasing it into the wild is necessary and desirable. But do this as incrementally and quickly as possible.

The competitive winner is usually the first one to get a solution to market. It's OK if you break things. Just fix them fast. Hire people who can move fast, think on their feet and don't mind a little chaos. Balance that with people who design well and think ahead. Reward them both and let both know that they are valued by the company.

Form Tiger Teams[45] to attack scalability problems and ask them to do great things. Let them know that it is OK to try seemingly crazy things and fail as long as they try again. Amazing innovations may result.

Corporate Culture

Corporate culture refers to the values, customs, traditions, and meanings that make a company unique.

---

[45] The term Tiger Team was coined in the US Space Program to mean "a team of undomesticated and uninhibited technical specialists, selected for their experience, energy, and imagination, and assigned to track down relentlessly every possible source of failure in a spacecraft subsystem." - Wikipedia

What is the company is about? How are roles defined? How are decisions made? What are the rituals and routines? What symbols, stories and myths about people and events are important to the company? As you scale, your corporate culture can help or hurt you. At the extreme, a poor corporate culture can keep a company from scaling at all. Here are some tips for creating a scalable corporate culture.

Celebrate

Celebrate everything good that happens in your business. Develop rituals as part of your corporate culture. For example, at Coherent Networks we rang a bell every time a software contract was signed with a power company. Everyone would gather and we'd tell them about the new sale and what it might mean for the business. In the web or mobile app world, each sign-up can be a source of minor celebration. One startup team set up an automated sound to play every time a new account is opened on their online service. When you hit a certain number or meet a certain milestone, have a party and set the next goal or milestone. These things are important, not just to keep people focused on the goal but and to make the business fun to be a part of.

Build Team Spirit

There's nothing more fun, in my humble opinion, than accomplishing something difficult as a team. The things we accomplish easily are easily forgotten. But I do remember meeting tight deadlines through all-nighters, struggling to get a piece of code to work, winning a deal that we thought was going to our competition. Through it all remember to laugh at yourselves and the *improbability* of what you are doing.

Through the years my co-workers came up with a lot of fun activities that had nothing to do with goals, but everything to do with being a team. Pancake breakfasts cooked on an electric griddle in the office, annual chili cook-offs, having the kids trick-or-treat through the office in costume at Halloween, playing softball, volleyball, golf, Frisbee and running in races as a team[46] all became part of the corporate culture.

---

[46]Team CRi in the "Corporate Challenge"

Chuck, Mark, Ken, Tom and Ed circa 1991 before racing as a team against other local companies.

There were also practical jokes galore played on co-workers which I am grateful to have been spared (mostly).[47]

Break Bread Together

Sharing food is a powerful bonding experience. You and your team should share meals frequently. When people work late to finish projects on time, provide healthy delicious food for them so they don't have to

---

[47] In 2002 I traveled frequently to Mulhouse France where the bulk of the Steleus team was located. I enjoyed exploring the Alsace countryside and sampling the remarkable gastronomic delights of the region on my many trips there. The French team liked to play a practical joke, taking out of town guests to the nearby medieval town of Egisheim for dinner. After dinner and a few drinks they'd suggest a walk around the town. It usually took several times around for the visitor to notice that the town's streets go in a circle!

Medieval Town of Egisheim

choose between stopping or vending machine fare. Great companies like Google understand the value of providing good food to their staff.

Sometimes significant issues can be solved over a great meal. For example, the difficulties of coordinating an international team (US, France and India) at Steleus were mitigated by informal dinners held the night before our Board meetings. These dinners gave the management team, the investors and the Board the opportunity to get to know one another as people and made working through problems together much easier. Because we had investors from both Europe and the US, we'd take turns holding the dinners and meetings in Boston, London and France. That gave us a chance to expose more of the team to the Board and also meant we sampled a wide variety of cuisines.

Healthy Competition

Some people can make a competition out of almost anything (e.g. most new users, fewest bugs, best design). If you keep it light and fun, pitting one person or group against another can actually enhance teamwork and performance.

Here's an example from Steleus. After one of our sales guys closed a deal in record time with the Central Utah Telephone company he challenged the other salespeople to close a deal that fast. We instituted the Elsbury Garlick[48] Award for the fastest closer. Miraculously, this shortened our average sales cycle as each sales person vied to top the others. The trophy kept getting passed around until the record finally peaked at one day!

Get Together and Change the Venue

As you scale you will need to create opportunities to get the team together to talk about strategy as well as to resolve issues. It's important to be physically together. I suspect that very few team-building or strategic breakthroughs happen on Skype calls. Even very small companies can have a strategic planning or sales meeting "off-site." When you are traveling anyway (to a trade show for example), schedule a few extra hours or even a day for a planning session.

When Coherent Research grew to about thirty people, we held a corporate retreat at Minnowbrook, one of the great camps of the Adirondacks. We invited the whole company and our outside Board members to attend. This event served three purposes: strategic planning during scheduled sessions, team-building through canoeing, hiking and games, and as a reward for the hard work leading to a successful year.

---

[48] Elsbury Garlick was one of the founders of the Central Utah Telephone company.

As your team grows larger, you may need to get together as a group in an off-site non-work setting once in a while to keep people pulling in the same direction. For example, by 2006 the Steleus teams in the US and France were well integrated into Tekelec and had grown to nearly $100 million in sales. But things weren't always smoothly coordinated when dealing with the other business units in Tekelec. Some problems simply couldn't be solved in the course of day to day business, so we organized a two-day meeting at Pinehurst Golf Course to work through the issues.

Off-site Coordination at Pinehurst[49]

These events take time away from work and cost money, but they can be vitally important to the company. When issues arise it is crucial to gain an

---

[49] Left to right, front row: Ron, Gabriel, Jim, Jeff, Dick. Back row: Lane, Chuck, Mark, Kyle, Nicolas, Mike, Eric, Doug and Steve.

understanding of others as people, to understand their challenges and remember that you are all on the same team.

CHAPTER 6 – END GAMES

"Every new beginning comes from some other beginning's end."
- Seneca

Let's summarize. I started out by telling you to go home and abandon the idea of doing a startup. Then I recognized that some people won't be able to go home. So by getting this far, you've self-identified with a group of startup addicts that can't help themselves. That means that there is no "why?" You just have to do it. Even if you can't stop starting companies, there is a point where each startup venture has to become something else. These transitions, or end games, don't have to be any more painful or difficult than the other transitions you've already been through.

For example, you survived the transformation of your original idea when customer feedback forced you to change. You synthesized this feedback and adapted the product or service to the customer's needs. You could have resisted, not listening to what your customers told you, and kept things the way they were, but that would have left you with no customers and a product nobody wanted. So it's the same thing when it's time for your startup to grow up.

There are many possible outcomes. Your startup's end game might be in the form of an acquisition, an IPO, a major funding announcement, or possibly a not so positive "flame out" – when the engines fail, you go into a spin, the wings fall off and you crash and burn. By knowing the realities of what lies ahead you can prepare to optimize the end-game and avoid mistakes that may cost you dearly.

Liquidity Events

Investors in your business are looking for a return. In order to realize a return, there must be a liquidity event when one or more owners receive cash in exchange for some or all of their equity interest in the company. To put it simply - cash for shares. The two main types of liquidity events are Acquisition and IPO.

Which of the shareholders profit from a liquidity event has a lot to do indirectly with the number and size of the financing rounds that have occurred prior and directly with the liquidity preferences of the various series of shares. Liquidity preference determines who gets paid first from the proceeds of a liquidity event. Series A (and later) shares are usually Preferred Stock, which means that holders of these shares get their money before the Common stockholders (usually founders, friends, family, accelerator programs and sometimes angel investors). A "1 times liquidity preference" means that the preferred investors get 100% of their invested capital back before any returns are distributed to other investors. Likewise a "2 times liquidity preference" means that preferred shares pay 2 times the initial investment before other owners see any return.

To further complicate matters, each new series of preferred stock often comes with seniority over earlier series. That means that the Series D liquidity preference must be satisfied first, then the Series C, the Series B, then Series A and finally, if there is any money left, the Common shareholders are "in the money". It can certainly be the case that when all the liquidity preferences are added up, there isn't enough money to pay all the shareholders.[50] The way to avoid this is to

---

[50] After acquiring the French software company, Network Management Group, we needed to change the management team, divest some significant non-core assets (very expensive and difficult to do in France), develop a new software platform, rename the company Steleus and relaunch the product in the US market. We had $20 million from the proceeds of selling Coherent Networks but needed to raise an additional $20 million round with a combination of Banc Boston Capital and GMT Partners. After

start fast, waste nothing and get to the liquidity event as efficiently as possible.

Acquisition

An acquisition is when another company buys a controlling interest (at least 51% of the shares) in your company. A merger is another name for the same thing. At the time of acquisition, what happens to you

---

building the business for four years, we sold the company to Tekelec for $56 million. When all was said and done we had Preferred shares outstanding from Series A to Series H, and combined liquidation preferences of over $90 million. The shareholder negotiations were complex and we went out of our way to be fair to all stakeholders. While not everyone was satisfied with the outcome I think we did the best that could have been done under the circumstances. The team got good jobs at Tekelec, the venture investors got a return on their investment and the management team got some restricted shares of Tekelec stock. Unfortunately because the liquidation preferences exceeded the sale price, the Common shareholders were not in the money (got $0).

"Tombstone" for the Steleus exit

depends upon a lot of factors, the most important of which is, are you still there? If you are not part of the senior management team, or not employed by the company at all at the time it is acquired, you will miss out on most of the potential benefits.

If you are present at the exit, you have a much better chance to profit from the event. First, if you are a valuable employee, the acquirer will want to secure your continued employment and should offer you a contract, possibly with some kind of bonus for your continued loyalty and contribution to the team. If the investors need you to help sell the company, they may offer you a bonus for your assistance in helping them find and close a deal with the appropriate buyer.

Going Public[51]

An initial public offering (IPO) is the first sale of stock to the public and the first listing of the company's stock on one of the public exchanges. Strictly speaking, an IPO is a financing event, not a liquidity event, and even startups with the option of going public are not necessarily better off doing so if they have the option to be acquired. In an IPO, upper management and early investors typically can't sell their shares for period of

---

[51] I don't speak from experience here. I have worked for public companies, but I've never taken a company through an IPO.

time and they take the risk the stock price might decline during this time.

From the company's point of view, the costs and burdens of Sarbannes-Oxley[52] compliance and the rigors of running a company in the public spotlight can be counter-productive for a company that still has to build market share. However, if going public is an option, a successful IPO can maximize returns for founders and investors and provide the capital for long-term growth.

Since the 2008 financial crisis, the technology IPO market has been very limited. In April 2011, Zipcar went public followed by LinkedIn and others in May and Groupon in July. Thus the tech IPO market seems to be opening up again. This is good news for entrepreneurs and investors alike.

A reverse merger is where a private company acquires a public company, usually for the purpose becoming a public company while avoiding some of the expense and time involved in a conventional IPO. This is only a potential liquidity event if some shares are also sold on the public market as a result.

---

[52] Legislation requiring onerous management liability for problems with public company reporting.

Less than optimal end games

Being acquired or going public are generally the best-case scenarios for a company. They are not the only cases however. To optimize your company's chances of a positive outcome I recommend that you:

- Are clear about your end game of choice. If you want to be acquired, build this into your culture, make sure that your core team knows it, and make this goal is a priority.

- Make a list of your target acquirers and decided how to position your company with them. Can you partner with them before you try to sell the company?

- You always need a backup plan. Make sure you are funded adequately for your Plan A to fail. When it's time to sell, it's best to be courted by more than one suitor.

Fire sale

In a "fire sale" the company is acquired, but at an unfavorable price or on poor terms. Fire sales are often brought about by investors exercising their contractual right to force a sale of the company in order to get whatever portion of their money back they can. Sometimes a venture fund needs to close its books, sometimes investors have lost interest in the company's vision, and at other times a quick buck simply looks better than playing out a different end-game. In a fire sale, founders and other common shareholders are routinely "pan-caked" (get nothing for their shares). Also, since the buyer is picking the company up on the cheap, they may not care much about the team or even the product.

Flame out

A flameout is an abrupt failure. Usually this term is reserved in the media for big failures, but a flameout can happen to any startup. No discussion of flameouts would be complete without paying homage to Phil Kaplan's 2002 classic book, *"F'd Companies: Spectacular Dot-Com Flameouts"* which chronicles epic fail after epic fail during the dot com bubble. Reading about other people's sketchy and grandiose plans going to hell via human frailties writ large is no doubt entertaining. However I believe that the kind of enormous cash bonfires described don't happen to most of us. The combination of greed, folly and self-delusion are not uncommon, but the scale of disaster described in the book is. So what about the rest of us more modestly greedy, foolish, and self-deluded folks? What could cause our startups to flameout? Here are six of the more common causes.

Failure to launch – lack of commitment kills a lot of companies. At some point it takes a leap of faith to quit your day job and devote yourself full-time to the effort of starting a company. That's easier if you don't already have a day-job. It's easier if you don't have a mortgage and car payment, much less college tuition or child-support payments. It's easier if you have winnings from a previous business to live on. But most of the time, success requires a period living on Ramen and sacrificing everything else to get a company going. Part-time projects while working at something else rarely if ever result in great successes. More often than not, when the going gets tough, the easier, safer day-job wins and the startup peters out. If you are reluctant to quit and devote full time to your startup, is it possible that you know on some level that it's not really worth investing your whole effort into it? Perhaps you should stop fooling yourself and devote full time to your day-job. Half measures rarely succeed in careers or startups.

Another cause of failure to launch comes from not wanting to do the necessary but unpleasant tasks. For example, coders want to code. Hacking is fun for hackers. Getting early adopters signed up and iterating on your idea in response to their feedback is only 20% coding. If you as a founder don't do the other 80% - the business of building a company – then who will[53]? Attracting users is just as important (if not more so) than building the product. To do so, you will have to do things that are uncomfortable if not down-right

---

[53] I made the naïve mistake in my first startup of hiring someone to handle the "business bullshit" as soon as I could afford to so I could focus on chip design. The person I hired was not a co-founder, but a paid President. I chose badly and the result was worse than no results. After about 6 months the fellow resigned, taking some embezzled funds with him which nearly killed the company. I recovered by getting my hands dirty and learning how to do the day to day business management myself. Once I made that commitment, things turned around.

unpleasant. Calling people, meeting people, public speaking, sending emails, tweeting, blogging and appearing in your own YouTube video are some of the ways of getting users. These are not exciting tasks if you're a coder or a hacker. But if you want your startup to succeed you have to do them. Or you can fail. Period.

Premature Scaling – launching or scaling your company too soon is one of the most common causes of flameout. It arises from a cognitive error, confirmation bias or preferring to listen only to input which supports your existing point of view. In the startup process, confirmation bias or "drinking your own Kool-Aid" manifests as thinking that you have market validation before you really do. Premature scaling compounds that cognitive error, resulting in inertia and waste. Remember, the number one predictor of success for an early stage startup is how many times it can iterate in an attempt to find a product / market fit and an optimal business model. No matter how you scale (e.g. hire people, cover more geography, add a new product or service), it will make it harder to change directions and slower to pull off an iteration. Inertia can kill you. Waste can be even more devastating, because the resources wasted (e.g. time, money, early adopters, press attention, people's patience) are generally non-renewable.

Running out of cash – How long is your runway? If your startup is an airplane trying to take off, then cash is the fuel for the engines. If you run out of cash before you're airborne, or even worse, right after you're airborne, well you get the picture. Every startup that isn't profitable has a certain amount of time left before the money runs out. You have that much time to either make it to profitability or raise another round of capital. The "burn rate" is how much fuel (cash) your airplane (startup) consumes in a month. The length of your runway (in months) is simply the amount of cash you've raised divided by your burn rate.

It doesn't matter if you run out of cash by raising too little or by spending too much. These are two sides of the same equation. One way to burn cash is to hire people before you absolutely need to. Premature hiring is a double whammy because it is not only expensive, but also has an inherent load – the need to manage those people takes time away from essential tasks (like iterating your prototype). Remember, if one woman can have a baby in 9 months, it does not follow that 3 women can have a baby in 3 months. But if you hire those three women, they'll definitely burn triple the cash in the 9 months. There are only two productive roles in the early stage – writing code and getting users. Hiring anybody to do anything else is probably a waste. The earlier you are in the startup process, the more dangerous waste is to your very existence.

Premature focus on profit – this one sounds like a paradox after we just discussed the problem of running out of cash. How can focusing on profit be bad? In the early days of the company, you're looking for a market that wants your product. You're also adapting your product to make it something that people want. Early on, you don't have the scale to deliver your product efficiently. So if you charge enough to make a profit early on, the price may deter people from trying your product and you may never find the market that really needs it.

How much market share do you need before you focus on profits? It depends. How big can your solution be? Are you trying to change the world or just solve a niche problem? How much money can you raise? Remember, until you are profitable, you'll have to raise capital to support the business. Get the product right first. To do so, you'll have to build a customer-base that gives you the feedback you need. Only then should you focus on refining the business model to build a profitable business. Getting this right is tricky. Get mentors' input on it and revisit the question often with your co-founders.

Raising too much money too soon – When you raise capital, you have to start spending it[54]. The clock is ticking based on the investor's time-horizon (often three years or less). Furthermore, you have to start spending the investor's money right away. You can't just put it in the bank against a future need. See the earlier discussion of Premature Scaling to understand all the problems this can cause if you've raised money too soon. The more money you raise, the higher the expectation of return, and the greater amount of board oversight you'll receive. Regardless of the good intentions of the board, having to explain to new board

---

[54] When I raised my first round of professional venture capital into Coherent Networks, this was a hard lesson for me. We received a $2 million A-round from St. Paul Venture Capital. We had a couple of big customers and had been profitable and cash-flow positive up to that point. In order to use the VC money, we had to give up the discipline of making money before we spent it. We had to take more risks in order to grow our business.

members with millions of dollars at stake how you need to scrap your product and start over based on the user feedback from your latest iteration is going to be painful and time-consuming at best.

Once you raise any capital, one of the founders has to manage the investors[55]. If you've got titles, it will be the CEO. That means sending the investors regular updates on how the business is doing, meeting with them one-on-one to get their input on every change in direction or business model, and asking them for help and advice. At the same time, don't let one or more investors run the company. Take their input under advisement, but make your own decisions. When things are progressing nicely, this will be easy. Very few boards mess up companies while things are going well. It is when you run into trouble that having managed your investors well pays off as you'll have a relationship and they'll trust you. If you've ignored them until a crisis occurs, the opposite is true, and the result could wreck your company. Generally, the more money you take from investors, the more time you'll need to spend managing them. Bear in mind, once the investors have control of the company (by owning more than 50% of the equity), they'll expect to *be in control.*

---

[55] I fell into a bad habit after raising a Friends and Family round. Since I knew most of the people who invested very well, I figured they'd just trust me to run the company. So I learned to ignore my investors. However when I raised VC money, my habit of ignoring them pissed the investors off. This is one of the errors that led to me being replaced as CEO of the company a few years later.

<u>Palace revolts and internecine battles</u> – When things get tough, and in a startup they inevitably do, the least committed founder often leaves[56]. This is traumatic, but can usually be survived, either by the other co-founders picking up the slack, or by recruiting a new co-founder with the right skills. Consider vesting founders' stock over 16 quarters so that if someone leaves early on, they don't leave with a big chunk of the company. Vesting is one of the easiest and best ways of structuring a buy-sell arrangement (kind of a "pre-nup" for founders).

A battle for control between committed co-founders is much more likely to kill a company. When this happens it almost always results in one founder leaving and one staying. If the one who "wins" turns out to be wrong, the company tanks. The one who leaves may also do damage to the company by starting a competing company or simply saying bad things about it publicly. Obviously this and other people problems are best avoided by picking co-founders carefully at the start. In the pressure-cooker of a startup each co-founder's character will be continually tested.

---

[56] I avoided this potential problem for more than 13 years; my co-founders and I stayed with Coherent Research and then Coherent Networks through all the incredible ups and downs. It probably helped that the other two were brothers, but mainly we got through by talking things out openly and honestly. In general I think three co-founders is more stable than two. It's much harder to stay stuck on issues if there is a third person who can act as the voice of reason for the two that are fighting.

Lifestyle Business

The term *lifestyle business* is a dirty word among venture investors because it means that they will not find a positive return on investment no matter how much or how long they invest in it. For this reason, venture capitalists sometimes call this type of company "the living dead." A lifestyle business is perfect for founders looking to create something long-lasting that will support them doing what they love. Running a charter boat in the Caribbean or a B&B in Vermont are examples of lifestyle businesses. However, there are few software companies and fewer internet or mobile applications companies that can succeed as lifestyle businesses. These fields are moving too fast. If you've found something worth doing on a small scale, chances are that someone else will come along with more funding, more ambition, better connections or better luck and make your solution obsolete[57]. A founder's desire for a nice comfortable lifestyle business will eventually kill most software / internet businesses.

Not every business can be or needs to be high-growth. If you prefer stability to change, it might not be right

----

[57] In 2000 I invested in a startup that had multi-user video conferencing in a browser before anyone else. The founder's insistence on moving from one government contract to the next kept this a lifestyle business and led to his company's inevitable irrelevance when Skype and a host of others passed them by.

Chuck Stormon

for you to start fast. It is no surprise that most venture investors avoid this type of business / founder. It is important to be honest with yourself and others about your intentions. If you don't want to take the company as far and as fast as it can go, then it is not fair to sell stock or pay co-founders with stock unless they understand the limitations you're putting on the business. That doesn't mean you can't raise money. It just means you have to be brutally honest in doing so. You can probably find partner companies who will gladly invest in your business because they see long-term synergy. But accepting venture capital at any stage will set up a critical conflict for a lifestyle business and thus should be avoided.

146

EPILOGUE

"Let us remember that, as much has been given us, much will be expected from us, and that true homage comes from the heart as well as from the lips, and shows itself in deeds."
- Theodore Roosevelt

This is a short book by design. I don't feel it needs a conclusion that "tells you what I told you" in the rest of the book. I'm going to use this space to remind you of four things. First, always do what you say you're going to do. Keeping your word is probably the number one predictor of success in business and in life. Make it a habit to under-promise and over-deliver.

Second, when you accomplish something, share the credit with the people that helped make it happen. You can't accomplish much alone. The more you succeed, the more important it is to acknowledge the help you had in getting there.

Third, be grateful for the opportunity to start and run a business and remember to have fun while you're doing it. There is no more rewarding pursuit I can imagine than starting and building businesses[58]. You should remember to be grateful for the opportunity to do so. Having fun and showing gratitude for people's commitment are as crucial to a building good company as they are to building a good life.

Fourth, give something back. There is no denying that the lot of the startup founder is fraught with difficulty, but *"this is the life we have chosen.[59]"* If I may give a piece of personal advice, cultivating a sense of gratitude and

---

[58] Throughout it all I have managed to work with people I like and respect, live where I want to live, provide for my family and work on things I am passionate about. I've traveled the world (e.g. UK, Ireland, France, Germany, Spain, Italy, Austria, Slovakia, Brazil, Colombia, Mexico, India, China, Thailand) and all over the US and Canada. Every year I learn more and grow as a person and a professional. I've been fortunate beyond belief or expectation and I'm grateful every day.

[59] As Hyman Roth points out to Michael "Don" Corleone in Godfather II.

actively giving back[60] are not only rewarding, but two of the best ways to get through the difficult times with one's sanity intact. No doubt you've learned lessons and solved problems that will be helpful to someone else. Offer that help and see if you don't get more out of giving than you expect.

Putting It Into Perspective

Throughout this book I've shared anecdotes from my experiences where I think they will illustrate the point I'm making. In case you're curious how these experiences fit together, I've included a timeline of the last 25 years. On the left are the companies I've worked for full-time and on the right are my investment (time and cash) activities. In the interest of space and to respect non-disclosure agreements, I have not included all the companies to which I've consulted, mentored or given advice.

In that time, the only non-startup company I worked for full time was Tekelec (which was a public company when it acquired Steleus). My contract required me to work there for one year, but I stayed for three. Upon leaving Tekelec in 2007, I began investing in seed stage companies while supporting myself through consulting.

---

[60] I attempt to give back by encouraging, mentoring, just plain helping and investing in other entrepreneurs when I can.

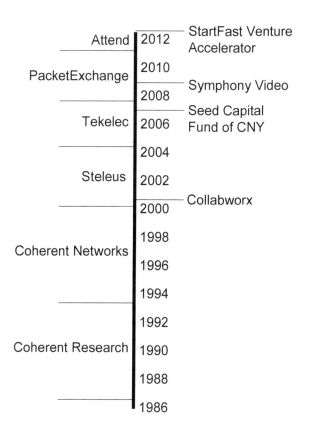

25-year Timeline

I soon realized that I missed being part of a startup team and in 2008 I joined my friend Rick who had become CEO of PacketExchange. For the next three years I worked with some of the best network engineers from London to Los Angeles for customers in the movie, television and advertising businesses. I felt a great affinity for these customers partly because they "get" my jokes, which are usually based on quotes from movies or TV shows. I also loved spending about a week every month exploring the beautiful and fascinating city of London where PacketExchange was headquartered.

I'd spent over a decade "on the road" including the year I was responsible for a team of about 50 designers and coders in India and was traveling frequently between there and France. Our partner in New Delhi, Vipin, organized adventures as part of these trips including celebrating the Indian holiday Diwali at his family home, trips to Jaipur, Udaipur and to some remote caves decorated with thousand year-old paintings inside. These excursions offset the difficulty of traveling to India.

Visiting Ancient Sites in India[61]

Coming Home

Earlier this year I joined a highly experienced post-production domain expert and a brilliant network

---

[61] Rick, Chuck and Vipin circa 2003.

engineer to co-found Attend which provides cloud computing services to media professionals. Attend is in the pre-seed stage and going through the exact process that I've written about in this book. Starting Attend felt like coming home again - literally because it is located in New York where I live and figuratively because starting companies is what I'm best at.

I also became aware of TechStars this year by meeting its co-founder, mentor and investor Brad Feld. I read Brad's book, *Do More Faster* and agreed with just about everything in it. I'd been mentoring and investing in tech startups for almost a quarter of a century, but I was blown away by the potential of the TechStars accelerator network. Here was a proven model to help entrepreneurs through a process I understood well and knew in my gut would work.

When Nasir Ali[62] and Martin Babinec[63] approached me with the idea of creating a TechStars Network accelerator program in Upstate New York, I was intrigued. After several months of collaboration the pieces fell into place for the StartFast Venture Accelerator, a member of the TechStars Network. We

---

[62] Nasir is executive director of the Seed Capital Fund of Central New York.

[63] Martin and Nasir co-founded Upstate Venture Connect, a not-for-profit that aims to develop an entrepreneurial ecosystem in Upstate New York.

will run a TechStars-style startup accelerator program for about 10 software, internet, or mobile app startups each summer for the next four years. Nasir and I will manage the program which is funded by private investors from around the state.

Nasir Ali

I can't possibly thank you enough for reading this book. My hope is that you found something helpful, useful or inspiring in these pages and that you Start Fast and have great success[64].

---

[64] Let me know how you're doing at www.startfast.net.

Notes

Notes

ABOUT THE AUTHOR

Chuck Stormon is a father of two and a serial entrepreneur with a master's degree in computer engineering. He has co-founded a chip manufacturer, a few software companies, an internet/cloud service provider and is collaborating on the StartFast Venture Accelerator.

Along the way Mr. Stormon has raised a lot of venture capital, been involved in significant exits, mentored a score of startups and invested in about a dozen. He frequently acts as a consultant to public and private companies on strategy, M&A and technology.

Mr. Stormon lives with his wife and two cats in Upstate New York, enjoying good friends and the abundant clean air and water, farm fresh food, trees, lakes and waterfalls.

18845968R00096

Made in the USA
Middletown, DE
25 March 2015